STREET LIFE

STREET LIFE
The Bryan Mosley Story

CHRIS GIDNEY

HarperCollins*Publishers*

HarperCollins*Publishers*
77–85 Fulham Palace Road, London W6 8JB

First published in Great Britain in 1999
by HarperCollins*Publishers*

3 5 7 9 10 8 6 4 2

Bryan Mosley and Chris Gidney assert the moral right
to be identified as the authors of this work

Scripture quotations are taken from the *Good News Bible*
published by The Bible Societies/HarperCollins Publishers Ltd UK,
© American Bible Society, 1966, 1971, 1976, 1992

A catalogue record for this book
is available from the British Library

ISBN 000 274021 4

Printed and bound in Great Britain by
Creative Print and Design (Wales), Ebbw Vale

Contents

Dedicated to the memory of
Bryan Mosley
1931–1999

Bryan Mosley's acknowledgements

Bryan wanted to thank his family for the love, help and support shown to him and Norma over the years, and particularly during the most recent times. 'My hope is that in sharing my life with you, my truly beloved reader, I am doing what God requires of me. For sweet you are, and God it is who loves you.'

Chris Gidney's acknowledgements

My thanks in the research, compilation and support for this book go to: Derek Ware for details of his long-term friendship with Bryan and his discovery and editing of the 'Polewheel' letters; Christine Gidney for her medical advice; Keith Mason for stories of the early years; Peter Byrne for details on the trip to France; the cast and crew of *Coronation Street* for making me feel so at home. Special thanks to Internet Corrie 'gurus' Graham Allsopp, Glenda Young, Chris Colcombe, David A. Hannah and Mike Plowman for their help and advice; Steven Sexton from the Diabetes UK Website; Ian Dickerson and Dan Bodenheimer from The Saint Club; Sally Goring for her trusted support; Dave Berry for that special friendship; Jan Korris for her counsel and insight; my publisher James Catford; my editor Kathryn Porter; and especially Trinity, my wife, and Luke, Anna and Ben, my family, for being the colours in my life and work.

My very special thanks go to my friends Bryan and Norma for all their tireless support for this project, and their faith in me to complete it against the odds. I especially enjoyed reading Bryan's own stories hand-written on the back of old *Coronation Street* scripts, which gave me a double amount of reading pleasure!

Foreword

I knew Bryan Mosley for 40 years. Meeting first as work colleagues at Butlins Holiday Camp, Clacton in 1959, we soon developed a mutual respect for each other's professionalism. Over the years this grew into the warmest of friendships. Indeed, it was a rare Sunday that one of us didn't phone the other for advice, an exchange of ideas, a gossip, a moan or a good old-fashioned natter, all of which included a couple of belly laughs. Bryan loved to laugh.

This is not to say we didn't have differing opinions, but somehow we always came to a compromise. He, like me, was a great believer that every problem had a solution. If you can't find a solution, then you haven't got a problem, you're stuck with a fact of life and therefore you have to live with it. On the other hand, he was not a man who would subscribe to the 'anything for a quiet life' philosophy. He had strong convictions which no amount of derision or cynicism would sway, most notably on the craft of acting and his accepted religion. I have always concurred with his views on the former and admired him for his belief in the latter.

When we first met I was impressed by his professional approach, with no background in show business, to the rigours of rehearsal, preparation for performance, characterization, and concentration on stage. Coming from three generations of theatrical stock (my parents were variety artistes, my grand-mother worked in touring Shakespearean companies, and my great grandfather ran a travelling fair) I had all the old tradi-tions of the theatre drummed into me from an early age, but was surprised to discover how Bryan accepted and carried out these tenets with such uncomplaining enthusiasm. This was before I realized how deeply he and his wife, Norma, were committed to their Christian faith.

This faith was, I believe, the bedrock for his existence, and a way of life for more than half a century. As a non-believer, I have often been bemused and, I admit, frustrated by his simple declarations of faith, but can never take issue with the fact that it gave him strength in many times of adversity.

Much of this may come as a surprise to those who think of him as being the bluff, blunt, bumbling and sometimes confused character he has played for more than 35 years. But Bryan wasn't always Alf Roberts. Forty years ago Bryan weighed 15 stone, was as solid as a rock and as strong as an ox. I know because I had to perform a live fight with him on stage. Three times a day we went at it hammer and tongs, me armed with an old-fashioned cut-throat razor and Bryan defending himself with whatever he could lay his hands on. As the set was a domestic kitchen-scullery of Victorian design there were many props and Bryan agreed to hit me with them all (including on some nights, I swear, the kitchen sink) before throwing me bodily through a window into the arms of the police outside. Surprisingly, apart from one backhand slap, the timing of which we never seemed to get right, I sustained no injury throughout the five months we performed the play. Bryan's secret was that, like his idol Oliver 'Babe' Hardy (the fiddle to Stan Laurel's bow), he was, for all his girth, light on his feet and could move with the speed and daintiness of a ballet dancer. This natural ability enabled him to obtain work as an actor-swordsman, theatre fight director and, under the pseudonym 'Buddy Windrush', a film and TV stuntman. Some memories of this part of his life appear in the following pages and I hope readers will be surprised and amused by them.

In pre-Alf Roberts' days Bryan was a sought-after character actor on the repertory circuit, for summer seasons, and in TV and films. I often think that his early casting in *Coronation Street* robbed us of a versatile actor equally at home in classic drama or high farce. He played a wonderful Porter in *Macbeth* at the Theatre Royal, York and I remember his entrance as the Reverend Mr Purefoy in *Sailor, Beware* never failed to get a round of applause. He was a convincing 'heavy' too, as anyone who saw him as the unscrupulous Brumby opposite Michael Caine in *Get Carter* will remember. My favourite performance of his was as a corrupt policeman in a Granada Television play entitled *Bent*. His understated menace was wholly convincing and the scene where he had to beat a suspect half to death was nothing short of brilliant. However, fate and duty towards a large family decreed his major role in life and if he hadn't created the endearing and enduring *Coronation Street* character of Alf Roberts, the public might not have enjoyed the series so much or taken Bryan to their hearts as they have.

In the transitory profession of show business it is not easy to establish true friendships or to keep them. Bryan, old pal, my life has been enriched by having and enjoying one of those rare friendships with you.

Derek Ware

Introduction

This biography takes a deeper, fascinating and humorous look into the life of one of the country's best-known soap stars. The lovable yet bland character of Alf contrasts sharply with Bryan's many off-screen experiences of great danger, excitement and drama.

Alf is not often seen to laugh, yet Bryan has been the stooge for many of the country's greatest comedians, so his story is never short of a smile. Indeed, his deep sense of humour, sensitivity and compassion for others caused Kathy Staff to announce at the end of Bryan's *This is Your Life* programme, 'How lovely it is to work with someone so committed to their faith as Bryan. He's such a lovely, honest, genuine man, and to work with him is a pure joy.'

Bryan has known both the shortage and the extravagance that the world can offer, but has found that his faith and his marriage to Norma have been the anchor in all of life's many storms.

1

'This is Your Life'

'He's the most famous shopkeeper in the country.'
Michael Aspel

With all the eagerness of a little boy at Christmas, Bryan sat down and began to open the newly delivered parcel. His anticipation was enhanced by the fact that he knew exactly what was inside. This package would contain an entire life of more than 50 years as one of the country's most popular television actors.

Bryan had been totally shocked and surprised when Michael Aspel, armed with this famous book, proceeded to interrupt him on the set of *Coronation Street*. Laughter and applause surrounded Bryan as he was whisked off to the nearby studio for the recording, still in a state of complete bewilderment. At home, several weeks later, the same laughter and applause echoed as the man of the moment unwrapped his memento. A gasp of surprise as the bright red album came into view, and smiles of delight as it was passed around for all to see.

It's been quite a life. Yet Alf, the grumpy, flustered buffoon we see on the small screen every week, is not the man whom his family and friends know and love. Bryan Mosley was born in Leeds in the summer of 1931, and has had a far more exciting life than any drama he has ever appeared in. Having been fascinated by the fact that Bryan was once a stuntman, I asked him what his favourite moment of danger was. Rather than picking a sword fight or a jump from a moving car, he smiled and explained in his matter-of-fact way how he was nearly killed in a plane crash while in the RAF. Bryan becomes uneasy when talking about himself, which is perhaps why he underplays everything. The most traumatic moments in his life are covered with an air of humdrum, almost as if he doesn't believe that anyone would really be interested. Like any good actor, however, his throw-away lines are the ones that are worth catching.

Bryan was born at a time full of excitement, changes and danger. An only child – unlike most of the families in the thirties, who had four or more children – he arrived in the middle of the Great Depression, just a few years away from the start of the Second World War. It was the year in which electric razors and reusable camera flashes were invented, President Hoover opened the Empire State Building, and Bella Lugosi first starred as Dracula. Bryan was a great fan of the early horror movies, and he remembers wetting his pants while watching *The Mummy's Hand*!

His earliest memory is much more ordinary, however, as he recalls the street that, despite the doom and gloom, was to become his beloved home. 'Whoever named the street I was born in must have had a rare sense of irony,' says Bryan. 'Rosebank View curved down a steep hill with not a rose in sight, and was a deadringer for Coronation Street. True, grass grew between the cobbles, and neighbours put out geraniums when the rain fell, but the rain was acid and inevitably killed off any plants exposed to it.'

His parents, Agnes and James Mosley, lived in one of the Victorian terraces that were very common in those days. The houses had been built to accommodate the workers for the nearby factories which had sprung up during the industrial revolution and which continued to belch out dense, black smoke each day. The Mosleys' home – 49 Rosebank View – was a typical Leeds house. With one room downstairs and two small bedrooms upstairs, it also had a cellar which regularly flooded from an underground spring when it rained. They were told by local health inspectors that the spring-water was pure and clean enough to drink, even though it could rise by three feet or more in bad weather. The whole street had been condemned years earlier, and by rights should have been torn down.

There was certainly no bathroom, so bath-night consisted of a full-size zinc bath being hauled out from an understairs cupboard and placed in front of the coal stove in the down-stairs room. Dozens of buckets of water were heated on the same fire and poured in. The water took so long to heat up that by the time Bryan was in the tub, he would be sitting huddled in a few inches of barely luke-warm brine. It was a real chore, so the easiest way to keep clean was to go to the local public wash-house, where it was also possible to do the weekly laundry. Agnes would often take the family washing down on a Friday evening, and the reluctant young Bryan would be commandeered to help push the overflowing pram of dirties slowly down the street, making sure that all the underwear was well hidden in the pile, to save any embarrassment.

Going to the lavatory could also be quite an embarrassing experience. Bryan would have to come out of his front door, turn left, go past the next-door neighbours' house and turn left again into the toilet yard. This contained, amongst the ever-overflowing dustbins, the small, whitewashed, brick-built hut that was shared with another family two doors down called the Bottomleys! It is a source of great amusement to Bryan that they never 'clashed', and he still has fond memories of sitting there shivering during the winter months, hearing the footsteps of passers-by in the street, and wondering whether his posterior was going to get frozen to the wooden frame.

At the back of the house was a short hallway which they jokingly called a kitchen. It was here that meals were prepared, except that there were no cooking facilities. Most of the cooking was done over the coal stove in the front room. It was quite an art and took a lot of hard work. It was later replaced by a two-ring gas stove, but even then the kettle was always left constantly on the boil on the fire in the front room, so that if a neighbour or friend made an unexpected visit they could (in the tradition of Northern hospitality) be offered some tea.

Despite the poverty, there was never any shortage of food. Bryan was sometimes allowed to cook, and became an expert in revitalizing the dried eggs which were common at the time. He remembers fondly that 'We had lots of pork stews, tripe and dripping. On a good day we would have ham and eggs for breakfast, but if I stayed at my Granny's, she would cook this incredibly stodgy porridge which I hated. However, she was an expert at cooking delicious and nourishing meals from cheap cuts of meat, augmented by potatoes, carrots and suet dumplings. Her rice puddings were fabulous, and her Yorkshire puddings were legendary!'

Bryan's father's parents, who lived at the other side of town, were like an additional Mum and Dad to him. They were all very close, and he would often sleep and eat in their house at weekends. The young boy was particularly fascinated by the huge mangle in the corner of the kitchen that Granny would use to do other people's washing. Granny did any number of jobs to make ends meet, and alongside the mangle she had various wooden 'dolly tubs' and 'possers' that were the early versions of manual washing machines. She literally had several irons in the fire, heating on the flames that burned whenever she could afford coal, and constantly ready to provide a well-creased finish to the shirts and skirts she worked with. For the many hours of manual toil she would receive just a few pennies, yet was always proud of her achievement as she handed over the crisp, clean pile of clothes, neatly wrapped in brown paper tied with string.

Fishing trips with Grandad were a regular outing that provided Bryan with an early taste for adventure. Piling into an old, open-topped charabanc especially hired for the event, Bryan would sit alongside other male members of the community. The vehicle's engine was started by means of a cranking handle inserted into a hole in the front of the radiator. It made a huge roaring and crunching sound as the engine turned, so that no passers-by in the street were in any doubt as to what was happening. As they trundled off along the cobbles, sounding more like a tractor than a bus, they bounced up and down like a set of woodentops, but it took only a few minutes to escape into the idyllic surroundings of the Yorkshire Dales. There they would find rivers abounding with fresh trout, which Granny would prepare and cook as an extra-special treat alongside Bryan's mother's home-made bread that she would send round whenever Bryan stayed there. One memorable day by the river, his father joined them and tried to spot fish under the riverbank. Leaning too far over, the bankside gave way and he toppled head-first into the stream. Everyone fell about laughing, but the reality of the situation was that his father's suit could not be put in the pawn-shop that week, so the family had to rely on the generosity of Granny and Grandad to feed them far beyond just a weekend.

The pawn-shop was a great benefit to keep the family financially secure when money was particularly tight. You 'pawned' some small item on Monday, and redeemed it on Friday if funds allowed. In this respect, James Mosley's one best suit was a valuable commodity, but where it regularly disappeared to was always a secret kept from the prying neighbours.

James Mosley was a portly man with a kindly face that seemed to suggest that he was ready to share a joke with you even if he didn't know you. An approachable man, he was an upright and central member of the local community, respected by all those around him, particularly by his only son, Bryan. James, known affectionately as 'Jimmy' by all his friends and relatives, went to work each day as a dyer's labourer. He was in fact an expert in his field – so much so that he was not called up for either of the two World Wars, his talents being considered of more importance at home. He was responsible for mixing up the many dyes to create exactly the right colour needed to turn pale new cotton into any colour required by a manufacturer. It was a very difficult process, with every effort being made to get the cocktail of costly dyes just right, thereby avoiding any waste. Too much red or blue dye could mean that the whole vat of bubbling mixture was useless. The working conditions were disgraceful, and Bryan is convinced that the constant damp and inhaling toxic fumes from the vats of dye contributed to Jimmy's early death. Bryan is still annoyed that his father was never properly appreciated for his skill or paid a wage that reflected his vast experience.

Jimmy's wage was one pound a day for a six-day week. Like many other men, he drank a lot, often spending evenings at the local Liberal club, the area's only real source of entertainment. As bouncer and treasurer, he was a trusted member of the committee. Despite his personal lack of money, he was never tempted to steal any of the hundreds of pounds that would pass through his hands each evening.

One particular night Bryan's admiration for his father was justified as he noticed his dad become increasingly worried about a pair of Army Commandos who had come into the club drunk. Wondering how his gentle and kind parent was going to handle this situation, he was astounded when Jimmy suddenly grabbed them and threw them out of the club. Following him out and down the front steps of the club, he was even more astounded to see his father give them a beating that resulted in two black eyes. Bryan was then enlisted to help take the men back home, where they were served a meal of fish and chips! The firmness and fairness that Jimmy constantly showed in all matters confirmed in Bryan's eyes that he had been lucky enough to have been given the best father on earth.

Even when the best suit had made its regular visit to the pawn-shop, Jimmy was always dressed smartly, complete with shirt, collar, tie and tie-pin. A waistcoat was an essential part of the outfit even in the warm summer months, and his shoes were polished every day. Most of the time Jimmy would wear a cloth cap to work, but 'Mam' would often make Bryan laugh by wearing his father's 'Billy cock' bowler hat, normally kept immaculate for weekends and holidays. One day Jimmy came home with his bowler hat full of sixpences and threepenny bits that he had won at the club. With a wide-eyed Bryan looking on, he asked Agnes, 'Do you want some money, love?' and threw a stream of coins all over the floor with the flourish of an instant millionaire who had just won the jackpot. For years afterwards Agnes found unexpected treasure hidden under the lino.

Agnes Mosley was an extremely attractive and graceful lady. When she went out she was often dressed as finely as her husband, although her collection of clothes was extremely limited, and often hand-made. She worked in several local cafés as a waitress, and tirelessly cleaned other people's houses after work and at weekends. Bryan was clearly valued, but feels that he took it all for granted. 'I was surrounded by love, but it is only recently that I have begun to appreciate that this kind of love is truly a gift from God.' His family's view of God at the time, however, was of a traditional, stern, biblical figure, and very much removed from the harsh reality of life in Leeds. Yet Bryan would say that his parents were 'God-fearing' people. His father was very much aware of the presence of God, but never put it into practice. Faith was something personal, it seemed, not to be shared or talked about unless you were in church for some particular ritual like a wedding or a funeral.

Despite the shortages that poverty brought, Bryan still describes his childhood as 'idyllic'. He was never lonely and never felt he was deprived, attributing this to the love and encouragement he received. His father was his hero, and the trips to the local toy shop served to enhance this image. Bryan loved toy soldiers, and Jimmy would sometimes tell him that he would buy him one.

'When we arrived at the shop he'd say, "Have one a' two",' recalls Bryan with a smile. 'I used to say, "Thanks – I'll have two!" It took me ages to work out that he was saying, "Have one of the two." Having won some money on a racing bet one day, he took me down to the shop and bought me a whole collection of toy soldiers. He would often go without his pint so that he could buy me something. He was very generous to me, considering how little he had.'

Being the only child meant that his parents would some-times be able to treat him to special occasions, even taking him to the theatre. Spending their hard-earned savings on some-thing that brought Bryan so much obvious happiness was a delight to them. Pantomime was Bryan's first real experience of the life that was eventually to become his own. These early feelings of the wonderment and magic of live theatre are still with Bryan to this day. The lights went down, the curtain went up, and a whole new world opened up in front of you. He was instantly and totally hooked. His great love was plays, and his heroes were the great actors and actresses of the day, like Sylvia Melville, Sissey Ashley, Frank Senior and Martin Carrol. Comedians like Nat Jackley and Norman Evans also fuelled his love of performance, and perhaps sowed the seeds of a liking for practical jokes which was to emerge later in his childhood.

It was a beautiful autumn morning when the small boy arrived at Burley Road Infants' School for the first time. A mixture of nerves and anticipation rumbled around inside the little boy as his mother led him by the hand towards this new adventure. He didn't have to walk far. Up the stone steps from his own house to the main street that rumbled with the sound of the cars and buses of the day. Mother and son said goodbye, and he was whisked inside the school hall by a kindly teacher clucking behind him like a mother hen. The whole school sang 'All Things Bright and Beautiful' in his first assembly. The motley collection of boys and girls from the neighbourhood watched eagerly as the new intake of anxious infants sang fervently, waiting to see if any of them were going to provide the familiar first-day puddle on the wooden floor. The tell-tale sign of wet trousers or skirt would always follow the culprit around for the rest of the day for all to see.

Bryan's bladder was firmly under his control, and he wanted to do the best he could and make his parents and grandparents proud of him. He already had reason to feel proud as he walked stiffly down the corridors in the new school uniform that his Aunt Mary had personally tailored for him. The majority of his poverty-stricken class-mates had no uniform at all, and had resigned themselves to wearing the same familiar time-worn clothes each day. Smart, short black trousers, grey socks and black shoes made the little boy stand out among his peers. There were no jumpers or ties, and certainly no boots. Boots were the one item of clothing that even his Aunt could not afford to provide. Yet a pair of black boots were an accessory earnestly desired by every schoolboy. Despite the lack of boots, Bryan was still better dressed than anyone else at his school, and he revelled in the feelings it gave him, as he shone like a shop mannequin among the drabness of his mates.

It was this ability to be well dressed which was to cause Bryan some early problems in his school life. Being seen as 'posh' by the other boys, he was quickly treated as an outcast and was picked on. He was bullied mercilessly, until he learned to avoid the bullies by jumping over walls and by changing his route home from school each day. Shortly after he joined the school, another method of levelling this apparent elitism was found.

He was shocked when one morning his teacher angrily called him out in front of the whole class. He stood there feeling humiliated before a whole sea of young, smirking faces. Several of the ones he particularly despised glared at him, and he began to feel as if he were standing there naked. Unable to make any sense of why he had been called out, or what he had done wrong, Bryan was totally confused as his favourite teacher stared down at him and frowned. Red and embarrassed, he fought hard to hold back the tears when Mr Halls suddenly produced his long, rickety cane from the cupboard. Telling the young boy to hold his hand out, Bryan half-closed his eyes in readiness for the pain. Mr Halls pulled the cane back high in the air, then brought it crashing down on the boy's open palm. When the blow came Bryan was astounded that he hadn't felt any pain at all, and immediately recognized a knowing glint in his teacher's eye. Quickly realizing that his tutor was holding back the force of each blow, his immediate response was to over-react as the cane hit again, pretending that it was the most brutal attack he had ever had the misfortune to experience. In the stunned silence of the room he winced horribly, his face creasing up with pain, and tears now filling his eyes. His performance must have been very convincing, as after about six or seven strikes he was sent back to his desk, and noticed with hidden glee the horror and sympathy on all the other little faces.

Amazingly, this moment of drama was to be a turning-point for Bryan, and became the key to end his struggling relationships at school. Immediately seen as a hero among his classmates for being incredibly brave, he was at last accepted and welcomed as a friend, even by some of his worst enemies. It is probable that the caning was planned by Mr Halls to instil some respect for the young boy among his peers, and maybe even to help bring the fashion-conscious Bryan down to their level. Whatever the motivation, it was something that many of his classmates would always remember. Bryan still receives letters mentioning the incident to this day. More significantly, Bryan had discovered a desire and a talent for acting.

Also, an unusual series of incidents was to encourage Bryan's newly discovered acting ability. It was as if Bryan's future career had already been chosen for him. One such occasion was the day when the school was visited by three smart-looking people from a local catalogue company. Arriving in the classroom, the 'spotters' immediately picked out three pupils, including the six-year-old Bryan, asking whether they would like to become models. He was flattered, surprised, excited and yet resolutely confident that this was the right thing for him to do. His parents and grandparents were delighted, particularly with the prospect of earning some badly needed extra cash. An appointment was fixed for the following week.

At the local photographic studio, the young boy was frightened out of his wits, jumping at any unusual noise, particularly police cars. His fear of these authority figures was not helped by the fact that his Aunt, who had brought him, seemed to get some pleasure out of scaring Bryan, often telling him that the police were coming to get him if he were ever naughty. But then the milk and chocolate biscuits arrived, which calmed his nerves. Then the suit he was to model was brought into view and was handed over for him to try on. The small child's eyes widened with wonder when he saw it. Made at London's Savile Row, it was expertly cut from high-quality material.

As he dressed slowly and carefully in the soft, white shirt, blazer and shorts it was as if he were entering a new world. Indulging in the feeling of donning a costume, it felt like he became someone else when he put it on, imagining he was the son of an army officer or an aristocrat. It was a perfect fit and felt good to wear, and because he was used to the quality, hand-made clothes of his Aunt, he felt very much at ease. This unusual confidence in so young a child must have showed, for as the number of pictures taken of Bryan in numerous different outfits grew, so did the family budget. Bryan's Christmas presents that year had an extra quality about them, and somehow once again it seemed that he was being prepared for an unimagined career that would leave his family and peers streets behind.

2

Street Life

'The only way to have a friend is to be one.'
Ralph Waldo Emerson

The front doors of all the houses in Bryan's street opened directly onto the pavement, and it was here that a big part of Bryan's social life was played out. It was a very caring community, everyone was open and friendly, and it felt very safe whenever you were out. The road often lay beneath rows of suspended washing-lines strung across the terraced houses, with items of clothing hanging like bunting at a festival. All manner of under- and outer-garments revealed much about the individuals who lived in the community. It was always a source of much acrimony when the washing had to be raised by a very long pole to allow the horse-drawn carts through.

Bryan remembers the carts of the coal merchants and the soap vendors. 'Gas lamps lit my street, with an eerie green glow on dark nights. The pavements were swilled regularly in a desperate effort to keep our street as spick and span as possible. There was tremendous pride in all the effort, and somehow people cheerfully coped with the difficulties of sheer survival. There was also a prison which I could see from my bedroom window. They still regularly hanged murderers there, and in my small boy's mind I was very aware that if I was too naughty, the same thing could happen to me! Interestingly, I could also see St Bartholomew's Church from my window too. It was like seeing the symbols of death and life all in one frame.'

The cobbles beneath the washing-lines were Bryan's playground. Every day after school and at weekends he played a version of football called 'gog-gog', using a screwed-up piece of newspaper tied with string as a ball. He was also becoming adept at imagining himself as one of the swashbuckling pirates he had seen in the films his parents had taken him to. With an old twisted stick in his hand, he would jostle and joust with all the other boys in the street and even offer to teach them the five basic movements that he had observed in films and books. David Poole was a particular friend who was always willing to join in the fun. He remembers Bryan as a wonderful teacher with incredible patience while trying to show him the complexities of swordsmanship. But Dave soon realized that he would never be as good as Bryan was.

While playing in the streets one day Bryan and his friends noticed two very well-dressed ladies coming towards them. 'We were impressed because they looked nice and smelt wonderful!' Bryan recalls. 'They asked us if we would like to come to Sunday school and if we had ever heard of Jesus. I had heard of Jesus, like at Christmas and Easter, and decided to go along and see what it was all about.'

His parents were delighted at the prospect of their son obtaining some spiritual direction in his life, and encouraged him to go the following Sunday. Although his family were not churchgoers, their profound belief in God had certainly sustained them in their difficult times. Bryan had been taught to pray from his early days as a matter of course, like brushing one's teeth each night. On occasions Bryan would notice how Agnes would often pop into different churches, though always alone. She never talked about her own faith. Like her husband, it was far too personal a matter for everyday conversation.

When Sunday morning came Bryan found that this new church, founded and paid for by local wealthy and committed Methodists, was to provide him with his first glimpse of God. The vast building, with many rooms adjoining the main hall, could seat nearly 500 people, and on this particular morning it was filled almost to capacity. As he sat on the wooden seats, which he felt were unusually comfortable for a church, and after a couple of rousing hymns, he listened carefully to what the man at the front was saying. God, he said, far from being removed and uninterested in his creation, cared and under-stood about everyone, and even knew all about the tough life of those who lived in the inner city. Bryan was enthralled at the thought of this 'down-to-earth God', and his fertile mind became a whirlpool of searching questions. He decided to go every week to discover more about this whole area of spirituality, which to his young, enquiring mind seemed far more exciting than life itself.

From that moment on, the Belle Vue Methodist Chapel became like a second home to him, and was to have repercussions which were to last through the rest of his life. Sunday school became a regular pursuit, and he joined in activities as often as three times every week. There were regular outings to local beauty spots, with glorious picnics of sandwiches and tea, and special parties and celebrations at Easter and Christmas. The annual highlight was prize-giving, when some of the rich benefactors presented the most diligent children with books.

The chapel was supported by a few very wealthy families who lived not far from Bryan's community. Mr Broadbent was something of a local celebrity, with a mansion set in acres of grounds at a place called Burley Woodhead, where Bryan and his friends would often be invited to go camping during school holidays and weekends. The boys never failed to accept his kind invitation, revelling in a world far removed from their own, where fresh air, space and peace filled their days. The enormous grounds seemed to go on for ever and were full of hazelnut and chestnut trees. Many wild mushrooms grew in abundance, but the city boys did not know which ones were poisonous and which weren't, so they steered clear of picking any of them. Vast numbers of foxgloves grew there and were eventually processed to make a useful pain-relieving drug. Mr Broadbent even had a full-size Maori canoe in a barn which the boys enjoyed playing with, launching it across the grass and imagining they were racing down the Amazon rapids.

Bryan was particularly astounded by the size of the house. He had never seen so many rooms and bathrooms. There was even a toilet where you could lock the door and sit in complete comfort and warmth! On his first visit to the house, one Sunday for lunch after church, he ran home to tell his parents that he had been unexpectedly invited to Mr Broadbent's. He described where the man lived and said he had two sofas and two grand pianos! They didn't believe him at first, and even scolded him for his over-acting, until he finally convinced them that it was true.

During those years at Belle Vue, Bryan became totally involved in the concerts that were an important part of the social life of the chapel. Bryan particularly admired the Lapish family. They were always there every Sunday and Mr Lapish led the Sunday school. He was a gifted comedian who often made his Sunday school class laugh loudly, and was greatly loved by all the children who attended his Bible lessons.

It was Mr Lapish who was the great influence in Bryan's budding acting career. The wonderfully comic characters that he created in his Sunday school shows would always be remembered by Bryan. One Sunday, when Mr Lapish was taken ill, it was Bryan who was asked to take over as 'Tambo', the leading role in the forthcoming minstrel show. Having already played the prestigious part of the front end of a cow (not the back end, he points out) in his school play, he was eagerly awaiting just such an opportunity to develop his talents further. In the time-honoured theatrical tradition where 'unavoidable circumstances' render the leading part up for grabs by the understudy, Bryan knew this was to be his first moment of stardom. Having watched his teacher avidly, he threw himself into the part, singing, dancing and acting his way through the show as if it had been his part in the first place. As the applause echoed around the tiny auditorium, he stood tall alongside his fellow thespians and imagined that Mr Lapish would have been very proud of him. It was much later that Bryan was devastated to hear that the whole family had died in a car crash, leaving Mrs Lapish to pull her life together alone after the tragedy.

Not surprisingly, the weekly Sunday school visits and the exciting activities did not keep Bryan from all the usual boyhood temptations. By this time he had moved up to Kirkstall Road Senior School. He had also joined the local gang. To be a member a boy had to take part in the regular excursions to the local shop in order to steal as many sweets as possible. Indeed, a weekly record was kept of who achieved the biggest swipe without getting caught. Bryan was against the criminality of it, yet he thoroughly enjoyed the sense of danger that was involved. However, Bryan's fear of upsetting his parents was a big enough deterrent to stop him getting into any serious trouble. He always remembered his father's advice: 'Keep your nose clean and you won't have owt problems, lad!'

Kirkstall Abbey, in Leeds, was to provide Bryan's gang with one of many extra-curricular activities. The twelfth-century building had a high tower with a very long wall, and one day the chums decided to climb over it. It was seen as a test of ingenuity by the boys in the area, as it was extremely difficult to scale, and most of them gave up quite quickly. However, from the top of it there was supposed to be a magnificent view of the surrounding countryside. This escapade was so terrifyingly dangerous that Bryan can hardly recall any of the details. 'All I know is, we climbed up one side, across the top, dropped down the other side, and scampered home in time for tea!'

Apart from building rafts to float down the local river, the illegal exploration of buildings seemed to be a favourite pastime for the group. Many of the houses in the area were very old and falling down. Some had even been half torn down by workmen, and then left derelict. The angular ruins standing defiant among the piles of deserted brick and rubble were, to the young Bryan's imagination, gateways to exciting adventures in ancient castles and haunted monasteries. Though forbidden to go anywhere near these dangerous places, Bryan would investigate each abandoned site with relish. Clutching their wooden toy guns, he and his friends would explore them, moving gingerly around the toppling brick walls. A favourite winter game was to hide in the dark, then jump out on a friend. This was a particularly scary game, as always at the back of their minds was the terrifying thought that one day it might be a policeman jumping out on them, having caught them red-handed in the act of trespassing.

One day it happened. In the half-dark of the twilight, as they were hiding behind some ruins, the boys heard a hearty shout followed by a lamp shining in their direction. They knew it wasn't one of them. None of them possessed a torch.

The officer shouted again and four very red-faced boys gave themselves up. One by one they appeared from behind broken walls like defeated soldiers. None of them could think of an excuse quickly enough to stop the frowning police officer taking their names and addresses. Bryan thought about his father's wrath, but then he thought about the extraordinary fun he had just enjoyed, and he smiled. He knew his father would not really be very angry anyway, and would more likely be secretly proud of his son's caper. This proved to be exactly the case when he was escorted home and handed over to a very bemused Jimmy Mosley.

The other boys had been visibly shaking and in tears, but once again, Bryan had somehow felt 'different'. He was buzzing inside with the excitement of the situation, sensing deep within him something that made him feel set apart from the rest of his friends. He had felt this way before – at school, when he had worn his new clothes, and when he had been picked to model for the catalogues. He recognized that the gang lifestyle was not really suited to him. He was basically a loner – he had his own bedroom, he enjoyed his own space, and he relished the company of his toy soldiers and cars. His friends could never compete with his own vivid imagination anyway. He loved allowing his mind to take him to exciting worlds far away where he fought in wars and drove cars at dangerous speeds. When his parents bought a wireless, Bryan's imagination was unleashed even further as he listened to all the plays of the day – though some of the more worrying tales like *Appointment with Fear* would stop him from sleeping at night, providing his mind with 'entertainment' that would keep him terrified for hours, until dawn finally appeared to rescue him.

For Bryan, it was colourful, exciting experiences that made life worthwhile. This is why holidays were very special to him.

They were often spent with Uncle Bob and Auntie Annie in the seaside town of Scarborough. The couple had just enough room to fit the family of three in their front room, with Bryan sleeping on the sofa. He remembers long, sandy days on the beach, eating mussels, shrimps and ice cream. He was always immaculately dressed, of course. He loved the beach and his father was a very strong swimmer. There was a scare one day when Jimmy decided to swim out to meet a boat that took people on sea trips along the coast. The boat must have been further out than he expected, as he was so far away that Bryan and his mother lost sight of him among the waves. Imagining that he had gone too far out to sea and was now exhausted, Bryan felt panic rise inside him. He screwed up his eyes and desperately searched for his father among the waves, when suddenly he spotted him again, working hard against the outgoing tide. Several others on the beach had noticed the preoccupation of mother and son, and began to cheer Jimmy on as he came into view. Bryan knew it was only his strength and experience that would get him back to shore safely. Finally arriving on shore, dripping with salt water and gasping for breath, he lay on the beach totally exhausted, and not a little frightened. Bryan was full of respect and admiration for his father once more. But Jimmy never went so far out to sea again!

The reality of war hit Bryan's street community like a bomb. 'I was on a fishing trip with Grandad's club. It was glorious weather, and the fishing was very peaceful, when suddenly a farmer on a shire horse appeared. "We're at war!" he bellowed, and we all decided to go straight home. Suddenly, down a narrow, leafy lane an ancient tank rumbled into sight and a Territorial Army sergeant leapt out to tell us again that war had been declared.' Somehow, Bryan and his friends knew that life would never be the same again.

When they arrived home everyone was talking about the news, and what effect they thought it would have on them. A few days later, as he was handed the awful rubber contraption that he would have to wear in the event of a German gas attack, Bryan began to wonder if all the imaginary wars he had stored in his head were about to come to life. The gas mask was kept in a small, square box which hung on his shoulders by a piece of string, and it smelt of old car tyres. It swung back and forth as Bryan walked, a constant reminder that one day it might have to be used.

The day to test out his new piece of equipment came when a large van pulled up in his street, apparently provided as a training exercise by the government. He and his friends were invited to step inside the adapted van by some very important-looking people in suits. Donning their masks, they climbed up the steps at the rear and in through the back door, along with some very worried-looking adults. There were wooden benches along each side of the van, and Bryan jostled for a space to sit among his neighbours. The doors clanged ominously, shutting out the daylight. An electric bulb emitted a glow like that of a small candle. It was a strange, unearthly sight that met the eyes of the teenager as he looked along the row of bodies waiting expectantly. With the two huge, glass eyes and the long trunk of the masks, together with strange and erratic gasps of breath from each one, he could easily imagine that he had been transported to some alien planet. Then a hissing noise made everyone jump. Smoke started to pour into the van from several small holes in the sides. Very soon it had surrounded everyone and was so dense that it was impossible to see the person next to you. By this time most people had had enough and were starting to knock on the door of the claustrophobic steel box, demanding to be released from this torment. Bryan, however, was not at all scared, and the experience only served to heighten his imagination once more. He was pleased to discover that his mask worked perfectly, but this did not remove the fear that one day it might actually have to be used.

While Bryan and his school mates were encouraged to play and familiarize themselves with their gas masks, they soon learned that the reality of war was far removed from their schoolboy's fantasy of what was going to happen. Rationing became a way of life, and many of Bryan's favourite foods became scarce and eventually unavailable. Bananas and oranges were hardly ever seen, and the weekly allowances of cheese and eggs were minuscule. Yet there was a wonderful sense of unity and comradeship that kept the community alive as people clung to each other in times of real hardship. Christian hope sustained the country too, and people shared the simple faith that all would be well one day, so long as everyone pulled together.

Many of the men in Bryan's community were suddenly gone, and the teaching staff at his school was now made up of older women and mothers. Because of his age Bryan just missed being called up to the forces, but he heard that many members of his family had joined in the great fight. His cousin Jimmy was drafted into the Navy, but his ship was sunk in Scapa Flow right at the beginning of the War. Jimmy was only 16 years old when he died. Bryan's other cousin was also in the Navy, and was stationed on the famous ship *The Hood*. He was on leave when the ship was torpedoed and went down with all his crewmates on board. He never got over the guilt of surviving all his mates, and remained adamant that he would rather have gone down with his friends. The loyal young Bryan understood this. Uncle Bob was called into the RAF as a medical driver and was eventually awarded two oak leaves for his valour. However, somehow his hair turned white within six months. Uncle Cliff was with the Royal Signals at the fall of Dunkirk, and was then posted to Singapore, which also fell into the hands of the enemy. He then found himself a prisoner of war under the Japanese in the infamous Changi Jail and worked on the Burma Railway. When he eventually arrived home at the end of the War he was a very sick man and died of beriberi a year later.

Before all these facts had become realities for Bryan, he experienced for himself the brutality of war at home. One dark night, he had just returned from his time at youth club when loud aeroplane noises immediately brought everyone out of their houses. The anti-aircraft gun-fire from the local ground stations echoed around the street, and red flares lit up the sky. He looked up to see the amazing sight of fighters engaged in a dog-fight, diving and twisting and turning in the sky. When shrapnel started bouncing off the pavement, it was enough to make them realize that this was too close for comfort. Without hesitation everybody started to run for cover, as the distant air-raid sirens began to wail. Some went to a home-made steel box under the kitchen table, while others went to a public underground shelter. For Bryan it was his grandparents' cellar. Unlike the cellar at home, theirs had been reinforced with concrete for just such an event as this.

When Bryan arrived the cellar was already full of petrified people, sitting huddled on the wooden benches. Some wore their gas masks and were unrecognizable; others were familiar neighbours. In the near dark, the flames of the oil lamps made strange shadows on the stone walls. Fortunately the cellar was not wet, but it was still extremely damp and cold. Somehow, as they sat close together, there was a sense of companionship and community. But no one talked – they just listened to the noises overhead, and waited. To Bryan it seemed that the gun-fire sounded like the patter-patter-patter of rain, and he refused to be as frightened by the situation as the others in the shelter were.

His thoughts switched to his father, who would be fighting the fires up above with the voluntary fire services. He remembered his dad telling him that he had recently dug a man out of a huge pile of rubble, finding him still alive under a tin bath with his Alsatian dog. There was also a woman who had been blown out of her downstairs bedroom and had been found buried, still asleep in bed. Another bomb further down his street had taken out Joe's Fish Shop and the Chinese laundry. In the darkness a bus had accidentally driven into the crater, injuring several people. Jimmy Mosley was becoming quite used to the trauma of digging for bodies after a raid. However, the bombs seemed to be dropping a little too close to home territory for comfort.

As Bryan filled the silent, icy moments with thoughts of what his father would be doing tonight in the streets above his head, he reflected on this good, simple man with deep complexities. Although he had no formal education, Jimmy was a well-read and very intelligent man, though, sadly, he was never able to put this understanding to any professional use. Taking a keen interest in his son's education, he regularly took Bryan to the local lending library, introducing him to many of the classic novels and great writers such as Major Charles Gilson and Edgar Rice Burroughs. He pushed his son to try Conan Doyle and Walter Scott, and eventually Tolstoy and Dostoyevsky. He was a prolific reader himself, and loved to discuss books by the fireside with his only son. Bryan had always been full of respect for his father, and even more so now, as he heard the continuing roar and wail of activity overhead.

Bryan's thoughts were suddenly shattered by a high-pitched whistling sound that came closer and closer at great speed. There followed a sudden silence, and then a massive bang, shaking the ground beneath their feet. This was followed by another, and then another. Many of the adults were saying their prayers, and Bryan could see the look of terror on their faces.

When the bomb hit the house, it was Bryan's father who saw it first. Unable to wait for the dust and mess to settle, and with tears in his eyes, he ran the several hundred yards down the road to where the row of terraced buildings had stood. Breathlessly dropping to his knees, he began anxiously clawing at the smoking rubble to dig the survivors out, desperate to know whether his own son was dead or alive.

But after a few painful minutes he looked up and realized that in fact the pile of shattered bricks was not his parents' house. The bomb had hit and totally destroyed a set of houses just three doors away from his parents' home. Getting to his feet, Jimmy turned to see Bryan slowly emerge from the front door of his Granny's home, shaken but still alive. As his father ran towards him, Bryan stared at the beloved street, which had become like a scene from another planet, with white sulphur from the explosion covering everything. Father and son embraced. It was the only time Bryan remembers seeing his father cry.

3

Underground Adventures

Consider the Turtle: he only makes progress
when he sticks his neck out.

Anonymous

Bryan's streets were equipped with all the usual shops of the day: Gratton's, the butcher; Bromly's, the greengrocer; Wilfed's, the hardware store; and, of course, Teemby's, the confectioner. The acute absence of money in the community meant that shop owners were not eager to provide their customers with goods 'on credit', for fear of never getting the cash. Everything had to be paid for at the time of purchase. The pressure on the shopkeepers from shoppers at this time caused one enterprising owner to put a broken clock on display in his window with a notice firmly announcing, 'No Tick!'

The War had caused a whole catalogue of shortages, which greatly annoyed the customers. More important for Bryan was the shortage of paper, which was a source of great disappointment to him, since he enjoyed creating and experimenting with his developing talent for drawing and painting. Bryan was a popular lad and was liked by the shop owners. It was Mr Gratton the butcher who delighted Bryan one day with a gift of a whole ream of paper to encourage Bryan's artistic talents. It wasn't until he got the bundle home that he discovered the quality of the gift. It was the sort of shiny paper that fish and chips were wrapped in – very difficult to draw on, but still like gold-dust to the young artist. After years of feeling guilty if any paper was wasted, these huge, empty sheets gave Bryan the tool to explore artistic extravagance once more.

He had excelled at Art and English at school, and now, at the age of 13, he was being encouraged by his teachers to apply for an Art scholarship. His grandparents were able to offer some financial help towards the fees, and so he soon found himself among the easels and oils of the Leeds College of Art. Bryan's memories of those days are of very happy and relaxed times, doing exactly what he enjoyed. Even the job of cleaning the brushes brought home to him how fortunate he was to be there. Bryan would say that if you want to be happy, take nothing for granted. Continuing on to higher education was totally unheard of in his neighbourhood. Most of his friends had gone straight from school to work in the light-engineering factories that encircled his community and specialized in making bed-springs. Bryan hated the idea of factory work, and was very pleased to have avoided it. He despised the expected industrial lifestyle of many around him and from early days was determined to be different. His parents had been somewhat apprehensive in allowing Bryan to break the mould in this way, but recognizing his commitment and dedication, they finally found themselves encouraging him.

Keith Mason had also won a scholarship to Leeds College of Art. They were in the same class at college, and Keith remembers his first impression of Bryan. 'He looked just like a bean pole. Being a very tall, thin lad, he was a fantastic runner – in fact, he used to run to college every morning from his home, which was about a mile away. I could never keep up with him, even if we bumped into each other on the way to college. He would always get there before me!'

Keith shared Bryan's sense of privilege about being in further education, and even joined the same youth club as his pal. Youth club was one event that Bryan never missed. Having spent most Sunday mornings at Sunday school, enthralled by the many and varied Bible stories that seemed to have a drama all of their own, he was now firmly established as a founder member of the club. It was led by a man named Eddie Reynolds, who was to have a great influence on the young boy's life. Tall and kindly, Eddie was still a soldier left over from the War and was posted in Leeds. His wife lived in Hull and ran his insurance business for him. Eddie became like a second father to Bryan as he challenged him, encouraged him and gave him his first proper taste of dramatics. In many churches at the time acting was despised and was even seen by some as anti-Christian. A quote from one essay published in 1890 still summed up the general view held by many churches: 'An Actor is one of the vilest vermin that hell hath ever vomited out!'*

Yet in the eyes of Eddie Reynolds the Christian faith and dramatics were perfectly at home together, and he would often stop the cast for a moment in the middle of rehearsals to enable them to reflect on the fact that God was with them, and was indeed the one who had provided them with their talents to perform. He also showed them how dramatic the Bible was, and pointed out that many of the parables that Jesus told were brilliant ways of getting an audience's attention and getting across an important message.

* Josiah W. Leeds, 'The Theatre: An Essay' (E. Hicks, 1890).

Eddie was also a first-class teacher, so everyone admired and respected him. This gave him the credibility to talk about his faith in and love of Jesus, and because those in his class liked him so much, they sat and listened attentively. A very funny man, he taught the youngsters how important it was to enjoy life, and his real love of Christ made them aware of God's closeness at all times.

It was during this period that Bryan made a commitment to embrace the Christian faith properly. He found reading his Bible particularly difficult until someone gave him a more modern translation. One of the first verses that Bryan took to heart was about raising your eyes to heaven and praising God. This was a spiritual activity that Bryan regularly did, and remained as a constant reminder of all the things he should be grateful for. It also fitted in with his concern to take nothing for granted.

Bryan recalls, 'I was so comforted by the fact that God was not an old man with a long beard sitting up in heaven, occasionally hitting us with a big stick when we got it wrong. Rather, he was a Father God who loved us, and who sent his Son Jesus to this earth for our benefit. Jesus was someone I could relate to as well because he ate, drank, walked, talked and went to the toilet just like everyone else. I also accepted that Jesus' ordained plan was to die on the cross so that our own sins could be forgiven and so that we could be accepted by God. I loved the way in which it was so personal, and I felt the presence of God with me wherever I went. I could talk to him all the time. It was a most wonderful time in my life.'

Bryan's great love of the youth club and his eagerness to understand the spiritual instruction and to practise his acting meant that he was by now attending almost every night of the week. He even became a youth leader at one stage. Sadly, it also robbed him of precious time with his father. Jimmy would arrive home splashed with the dirt and dye of the factory, literally passing his adolescent son on the doorstep on the way to his beloved club. Most young people will naturally take their parents for granted, but even today deep regrets of passing his father at the front door like this will quickly move Bryan to tears.

The natural development from the youth club was the Scouts, and Bryan was very proud to be part of this movement, which taught him survival skills and a determination to get through the hurdles of life. It also gave vent to his inclination for boyish fun. For Bryan's greatest delight was giving new boys at the College of Art his own initiation ceremony. With Keith Mason, who was also a Scout, and other college mates, he would lead the fresh, worried-looking boys blindfolded down to Leeds Canal. Bryan would tell them that the ceremony involved throwing them into the canal to see if they could swim. They would be made even more frightened when an outside tap was used to make the sound (and often the reality) of nearby water! Then the boys would suddenly run off, leaving the blindfolded and bewildered youngsters still standing there.

Another favourite trick was to hover outside Lewis's department store in Leeds, looking up into the sky. After a while the boys would move away, leaving a small crowd of passers-by, all looking up into the sky, not knowing what they were expected to see.

Keith Mason remembers that one day the Scouts were asked to help down at the local church. 'We were asked to do some decorating by the Scoutmaster, Mr Deedy. He showed us into one of the rooms and, giving us some old tins of paint which had been donated to the church, he asked us to paint the room white. With sneaky schoolboy grins on our faces, we all looked in Bryan's direction. He suggested that we not only paint the walls white, but everything else as well. The sink, the cupboards and even the furniture were left dazzling after two hours of our efforts. When he returned the Scoutmaster couldn't believe his eyes, but we had to come back and scrape the paint off the windows later!'

In order to support Keith's desire to win a Scout award, Bryan agreed on a camping trip into the country for a few days. 'Getting the tent up wasn't easy, as it was an ex-Army tent with no instructions and some vital bits missing. Somehow Bryan managed to get it to stand on its own, though we were worried that one breath of wind might send it sailing through the air. I was interested to see how good Bryan was at self-preservation. He seemed to know how to make himself comfortable, and I watched as he prepared his sleeping arrangements with one blanket underneath and one on top. He was as warm as toast while I froze.'

Bryan's sense of self-preservation was seen in every part of his life, even in problems encountered with his acting. For the boys the highlights of the Scouting year were the Scout shows, which brought an immense amount of satisfaction to Bryan. On one particular occasion he was due to exit stage left and was supposed to return with a plate of food to set down on the table in front of his pal. Having got into the stage wings, Bryan could find the plate but no food. It had not been re-set after a previous performance. Aware that his fellow actor was now ad-libbing furiously on stage in order to cover the silence, Bryan grabbed the first thing he saw and placed it on the plate. This was a large metal hammer, and, wandering back on stage, he placed the plate on the table and said to Keith, 'Sorry, but it's gone a bit hard!'

31

They would also do their version of Scott & Whaley, a famous minstrel song-and-dance double-act of the day, using dark make-up to 'black up'. They were able to copy their heroes' routines exactly, and even got the same laughs in the same places as the famous duo themselves.

It is ironic that Bryan's regular weekends away with the Scout group were to cause a steady decline in his church attendance. When he was asked to speak at a forthcoming youth service he declined on the basis that God was not only to be found inside church, but in the big, wide world too. For Bryan, God was as real to him on the Yorkshire Moors as he was in the inhibiting atmosphere of the local chapel. 'I suppose I started to fall away from religion, but not from God himself,' says Bryan.

With Bryan's love of Scouting, it is perhaps understandable that the one thing that made him feel below par among his peers was the missing Scouting boots that most of his better-off mates possessed. They were the one item of clothing that he had missed out on at school, and now he desired them more than ever. He often mentioned this to his father, but always recognized that this was the one item of the uniform which was the most expensive, and he knew that the chances of him ever getting a pair were pretty slim. Little did Bryan know, but his father had already begun putting money secretly aside so that he could eventually purchase some for his son. When later confined to bed with a severe case of lumbago, his father apologized for not being able to buy him the boots that he so desperately wanted, and implied that he might not ever be able to do so, due to the fact that he could not earn a wage while he was ill. Bryan, very touched by his father's admission of helplessness, and never one to complain or protest, decided to go pot-holing instead.

Boots were not required for pot-holing, but strong nerves certainly were. Bryan had been invited along by several of his college mates, and they had agreed to meet at a specific spot in the Dales to begin their adventure. It was a summer activity and would involve a whole day when there was no college. 'Little Hunt' began with a vertical shaft that plummeted more than 60 feet down into the blackness. The adjoining shafts ran horizontally under the rock, like a huge rabbit warren. The tunnels had been cut into the solid limestone over many centuries by an underground river which started its journey on the surface several feet away from the open shaft. It was essential that the river was blocked up as much as possible so that the boys had as long as necessary underground without the water overflowing into the subterranean chambers and flooding them. They set to work finding logs and stones with which to make an effective dam. With the river above ground successfully stopped, they knew that it was safe to venture into the caverns – so long as it didn't rain, of course.

One of the team had come up with the brainwave that is still used by some pot-holers today in these particular circumstances. Into the river above ground was tipped a solution of harmless dye so that if the river started to overflow, those below would notice the change of colour in the water as it ran through the tunnels, warning them to return to the surface as soon as possible. One of the team of five teenage boys was elected as the lookout, and would be able to alert the authorities if there were any mishaps or if the boys had not returned by the agreed rendezvous time. Several of the team were experienced and trained in the art of pot-holing, but this made it no less dangerous. Bryan excelled himself in his excitement as his heart thumped in anticipation of getting below ground.

As the lookout looked on, one by one the boys descended the shaft by means of the simple rope ladder, its end tied firmly to the nearest rock. Last but one, Bryan stepped into the black hole and step by step began to descend into the chasm, wondering what would happen if the ladder broke. He quickly pushed the idea out of his mind when he felt the sudden drop in temperature. The hole was barely two feet wide, and it was impossible to turn around in it. At the bottom, he looked up to see the last boy beginning his own descent down the chimney, and he heard the clear shout from the boy in front to follow him down one of the tunnels. Shining his torch ahead of him, he could see a long passageway similar to the shaft but almost perfectly horizontal. It stretched away from him like the throat of some huge monster, and he started to crawl on his belly, trying to catch up with his mate ahead, whom he could see silhouetted against the light of the boy's own flashlight. The water trickling along the floor of the tunnel was immediately soaked up by the layers of old clothing that he was wearing, and he quickly became wet through.

As he snaked his way through the narrow cavity, there was no hint of claustrophobia. He was savouring every moment. Very soon the tunnel led to a cavern, and as they shone their torches into the darkness, their beams hit hundreds of stalactites and stalagmites. Bryan was full of wonder at the opportunity to visit this secret place beneath the ground, and his mind filled with vivid images from the pages of Jules Vernes' book *Journey to the Centre of the Earth*. Suddenly there was a shout, and Bryan looked down to see the water beneath him flowing faster, and with a strange tinge of red.

Obviously, torrential rain had caused the blocked river to overflow and cascade down the many recesses and into the chamber where the boys were now huddled together, considering their next move. It was too far to get back to the surface quickly, and too dangerous to slide along any of the tunnels, as it was possible that they could suddenly gush like a tap at any moment. There was only one solution, and one of the more experienced boys ordered his team to climb onto one of the ledges along the side of the cavern, to await the easing up of the rain, and to avoid the rapidly rising water.

Despite the fact that they were trapped, soaked through and in danger of drowning, there was no panic. Indeed, this seemingly terrifying scenario was quite normal for this particular area, and all the boys chattered and laughed as they clung to the side of the rock and waited. An hour or so later, when Bryan's legs were beginning to tire, the leader of the group said they should now return to the surface. Not only had the water level subsided, but it now contained a blue hue, caused by the dye placed in the water by the lookout above as the 'all clear' signal that the rain had finally stopped. Slithering back along the nest of tunnels and collecting the mud and slime that the water had washed into the narrow passageway, Bryan finally reached the bottom of the main shaft and began his ascent up the rope ladder once more. Well before he reached the top, the daylight invaded the vent with increasing brightness, until, reaching the aperture, Bryan found that he could hardly keep his eyes open, blinking as if he had just emerged from his beloved cinema. It was an adventure that he never forgot, and it left him with a definite hunger for more.

4

Life in the Services

'It makes me shudder when I think
my life could have ended so early.'

Bryan Mosley

There was a tremendous sense of relief in the community when on 11 November 1945, the War was finally declared to be over. Even with the end of the War, there were still many hardships to endure as Britain was plunged into an economic depression. For Bryan it was also the year when he left the Art College that had played such a big part in his life. It had introduced him to real freedom and had enabled him to explore his own artistic talent. One adventure was now over, but a new one was about to begin.

Bryan remembers vividly that the winter weather of 1946 matched the mood of the country. 'The snow stayed deeply frozen in the streets, sometimes shoulder high, until almost April. I quickly got my first job in a studio making papier-mâché items for shops with a firm called Northern Art Industries. I even did some scenery for the Christmas grottos that year, but found the job generally unexciting.'

He soon left to work for a firm which made playing cards and the millions of glossy labels for tins of soup and other foods, some for famous brand-names like Cross and Blackwell.

The thought of working there actually appalled him, with visions of early starts, tram journeys to get there and clocking in, which would play havoc with his outings to the cinema and his amateur acting. Hoping to get into the Art Department, he took on a job as an apprentice guillotine operator, which meant spending his days cutting labels to extremely precise sizes. The drudgery of it made him very restless, and he constantly battled against the feeling that he was slowly stagnating. After a while, as there still seemed no opportunity to move up into the Art Department, he decided that he had had enough and wanted to leave, but was unsure how to put this into effect.

For deep within Bryan was emerging a hunger for something else. Something that was more rewarding and definitely more exciting. It was becoming painfully obvious to his friends that the thrilling feelings of fulfilment that he had experienced in amateur dramatics made him feel constantly unsatisfied and unsettled in every aspect of his working life. His evenings and weekends at the local drama society were all-important to him, and it was here that Bryan was to meet Peter O'Toole. A tall, dashing lad, Peter shared Bryan's feelings of being trapped in a dismal career, and suggested to Bryan that they both become professional actors. This was an impossible dream as far as Bryan was concerned, and it only heightened his feelings of frustration. The thrill of the theatre just could not be matched by anything else he did, and it was this bubbling discontent that was to cause him to move jobs so often.

This constant search for something new and challenging, coupled with his increasing unwillingness to conform in the Guillotine Department, eventually caused him to be sacked from the company. Bryan found himself not only out of work but also at loggerheads with his parents. They were horrified when he was sacked, exclaiming that 'A job with Alf Cooke's is a job for life, lad!' They felt that he had just lost a great career for no particular reason. One suspects that Jimmy wanted his son to have a secure job with good opportunities for promotion – the kind of job he had never had himself. Despite regretting the pain he caused his father by the arrogance that he showed at this time, his determination to find the job that suited him remained.

Despite leaving Alf Cooke's without another job to go to, it wasn't long before Bryan found employment at Mowbray's bookshop, where he was encouraged by the manager, Mr Bridgen, to pursue his amateur acting activities. This under-standing of Bryan was stretched to the limit, however, when the young man's passion for books compromised his ability to serve the customers. They were left waiting while Bryan hid behind the shelves, hungrily reading! The manager's patience finally snapped. He decided that he could not cope with his assistant's 'dreaminess' any longer, and so Bryan was unem-ployed once more.

Another chance to test out his capacity to sell came a few weeks later when Bryan was offered the chance to join a busi-nessman friend selling clothes on a door-to-door basis. At least this work was more of a challenge. He worked on commission, and sold anything from men's suits to ladies' underwear, earning a shilling for every pound's worth of clothes he sold. He also sold books and collections of encyclopedias, though these were more cumbersome to carry and caused him much frustration. Surprisingly, Bryan found this form of selling quite easy, but refused to be pushed into the hard-sell scenario that his colleagues often adopted. On one occasion Bryan sold a set of books to a family whom he knew could not really afford it. He offered to take the books back and told the family that if they really wanted to know what was inside, they could read them all for free at the local library!

The most enjoyable part of the job was the opportunity to meet so many different people of all ages and of every background and class. This was to be an invaluable tool in his acting career. Years later, when trying to 'build' a character, he would refer back to some of the personalities he had met during this period of his life.

It was his salesman friend who inspired Bryan with an idea of how he could find the excitement he was earnestly searching for. Having been in the Air Force during the War, he would recount to Bryan stories of heroics and fun that sent Bryan's mind into action once more. He told Bryan that if he was ever called up, he should join the RAF and ask to be put in air traffic control, because it was a prestige job. Bryan loved the thought of wearing the uniform and was besotted with the drama of the Battle of Britain. So, shortly after turning 18, he joined the RAF as part of his National Service.

Bryan recalls that 'On 15 December 1949 I kissed everyone goodbye and was sent to Padgate, a grim training camp near Warrington, Cheshire. I was kitted out in my new RAF uniform, given an armful of jabs for typhoid and smallpox, and then immediately sent back home on Christmas leave! My Dad was very proud of my uniform and took me straight down to his club to show me off. I felt great!'

The blue uniform which Leading Aircraftman Bryan Mosley now wore continuously was obviously a good prop, not just because it reminded him of the theatrical costumes he loved to wear, but also because it attracted girls. The opposite sex had not played much of a role in Bryan's life until now. Some adolescent fumbling behind bushes while on a day's hike with friends was really the sum of his experience in this area. He had already met Norma when he was just 12. He fell hopelessly in love with her and consequently compared every girl he met with her. Even Barbara, a long-time girlfriend whom he describes as the apple of his eye, was no match for the feelings for Norma that he kept buried deep within him.

Any girlfriends that Bryan did take out were very likely to have ended up at the local cinema. Not in the back row with the lights down, as they might have expected or even wanted, but near the middle, with Bryan on the edge of his seat, focused on every move, every word, every nuance. He loved the cinema with avidity. It showed him life beyond his own experience and gave him aspirations and dreams. Some of those films made such a deep mark on Bryan that they still move him to tears today. His great hero was the swashbuckling ladies' man Errol Flynn. He loved the way this master of action ducked, dived and swung in the Hollywood epics of the day, and fervently wished himself in Flynn's shoes. Laurel and Hardy were also firm favourites. Bryan loved their comic antics, and if he could have chosen to be born as anyone else right there and then, he would have wanted to be Oliver Hardy.

The Hollywood film factory kept Bryan enthralled, whatever the film. He had a deepening desire to be part of this wonderful profession. During one of these visits to the cinema Bryan decided that he was in the wrong job. All the years of frustration and struggling had finally brought him to this obvious conclusion. He would never find true happiness in anything else and must seriously pursue a career in performing. The only problem with this was that he had two years of service in the RAF ahead of him.

Saying goodbye to his family once more, Bryan embraced his father. Their time together had been special, and Bryan felt he was getting closer to his Dad again. They had shared many good times together while Bryan had been on leave. Only one thing had disturbed him. Jimmy had asked Bryan to make sure that he would always look after his mother, if anything should happen, as she was unwell at the time, supposedly suffering from some unknown disease. Bryan was perplexed by this request but agreed to his father's wishes, and set off down the cobbles.

Arriving back at base in the New Year of 1950, he volunteered for Aircrew and was posted on to Hornchurch in London. There were 70 conscripts, and only one lad, who had been at Eton, was accepted for a short-term commission. Everyone else had to endure two years of rough training. Bryan was offered a course as a navigator, with a posting to either Canada or Southern Rhodesia (now Zimbabwe). The snag was that he would have to sign on for three years, which he didn't fancy, so he declined and was sent back to Padgate.

Bryan says that winter at Padgate was very cold. 'We learned to steal coke to put on the iron stove in our dormitory. The food in the service canteen was so disgusting that it was inedible, and there was never enough, so we always left feeling hungry. It meant that we stole bread, potatoes and carrots wherever we could. We toasted the bread and roasted the spuds on the stove, and filled up on raw carrots. I learned later that this deprivation had been done on purpose as part of our survival training, presumably in case we were captured by the enemy!'

The basic training continued with Bryan being shown how to kill, how to use a gun and how to march for hours on end. They were also taught many tricks of the trade such as polishing uniform buttons with brown sauce. This was also the time when he had his first experience of riding a bicycle, since his parents had never been able to afford to buy him a bike. He offered to take a letter down to the post-box for a friend, and the bike was loaned to him so that he would get to the post-box in time to catch the last post. Bryan, in his usual confident manner, and unwilling to confess that he had never ridden a bike before, climbed aboard and set off at an alarming pace as if he did it for a living. Surprisingly, he never fell off!

While on a training exercise one day, Bryan was ordered to go and see his commanding officer at once. Entering the small, bare office, he stood to attention before the desk. An ominous silence filled the room, and Bryan could see that the CO was contemplating what to say. Bryan suddenly thought of his mother. She had been quite ill when he last saw her. He remembered that his father had even warned him, so Bryan prepared himself for the worst. Staring Bryan straight in the eye and taking a short, deep breath, the officer quietly walked around the outside of the desk and stood in front of his airman. 'I'm sorry to have to bring you some bad news. I'm afraid to have to inform you that your father died this morning. I'm very sorry.'

The force of these words hit Bryan's mind like a bullet. He was struck dumb. This was not what he had expected at all, and at first he struggled to take the information in. As if hoping that the CO would turn round and tell him it was not really true, he stood to attention for several moments, staring straight ahead, before collapsing into a nearby chair. He was totally devastated by surprise and shock. His beloved father and friend was gone. He hadn't even had a chance to say goodbye, or to be there for him. Feelings of guilty torment were added to the loss he felt. An empty blackness rose up inside his stomach and filled his throat, causing it to knot up. Eventually several other airmen were called to help Bryan back to his dormitory to recover. Bryan wondered if he ever would.

Immediate compassionate leave was granted, and the young airman collected his things and took the long train journey back to Leeds. Regrets that his father had died before he had been able to repay him in some way for all his kindness over the years caused Bryan to weep constantly as the countryside sped by. Carrying the deepest sorrow that he did not walk to work with Jimmy on that final day of leave, he was mindful that this was the last time he had seen him alive. His thoughts drifted to his times at the youth club, and the wonderful Eddie Reynolds, whom he had now lost contact with and missed so much. Happy memories of his youth flooded back with a vigour that surprised him. Being a nostalgic man, thoughts of the past that he now considered lost just brought forth more choking tears.

Arriving home, he was met by his mother and grandparents, who were all in a dreadful state of shock. The doctors thought his father had died of a heart attack. The family had been totally unprepared for this tragedy, since Jimmy was just 46 years old. The grief that Bryan felt over his father's death was a terrible experience, and it didn't seem to ease. It had shaken him to the core, with the result that during those few days at home he spent most of his time speechless and alone. He didn't know what to say, and preferred his own company at this time, taking long walks onto the Moors. He felt bereaved and lonely, and was unsure about what was on the road ahead.

The funeral was a very sombre occasion. As the horse-drawn hearse stopped outside his father's Liberal club as a mark of respect, Bryan sensed that his own life was about to change dramatically. If it wasn't, then he must make sure it did. As the desire to leave the past behind became more acute, so the determination to succeed in his new chosen career increased. He decided to get back to Padgate as soon as possible.

Everyone at the camp was supportive and, despite suffering what he describes as an 'emotional breakdown', possibly brought on by locking in his grief, somehow Bryan managed to get through the very hard basic training that followed. His best pals literally carried him through the passing-out parade that celebrated the completion of their training. His 'Mam' was invited to the ceremony, and Bryan was disappointed that she didn't come, apparently because she didn't have enough money for the train fare. Bryan compensated by going home most weekends to make sure she was properly cared for, as his father had asked him. This made most of his billet-mates envious, and when one of them made a stupid comment about his mother, Bryan became incensed. He attacked the other airman with an aggression that he had never experienced before, grabbing him by the arms and pulling him down on the floor in a wrestle. Bryan was much stronger than the other young man, who realized quickly that he was no match for Bryan, and tried to pull back. Because they had both been trained to kill, the fight got more and more out of control, until Bryan was on the point of hitting the other man in the throat in such a way that it would have killed him instantly. It was an instinctive action that suddenly frightened him and brought him quickly to his senses. For one crucial moment he had lost control. Realizing the power he had and what damage he could have done, he stood up and walked away from the writhing, sobbing mass on the floor. The pair could easily have been punished, but nothing was said, and remarkably, both airmen stayed friends afterwards.

From that day on, Bryan began to hate the thought of being trained to kill people, and dreamed of the possibility of making people laugh instead. It still remained a dream, though. Any thoughts of going into the theatre professionally had always been instantly brushed aside by family and friends, and particularly by his father. He had been told by Jimmy that you needed a lot of money to go into the theatre business. 'They are all well dressed and speak properly – nothing like you!' he would say discouragingly. Now that his father was gone, Bryan felt a new sense of freedom and a new sense of destiny.

It was this increased self-confidence that helped Bryan to survive one of his most traumatic moments in the RAF. One wonders if the way in which he was sent from pillar to post was in itself a training for the years of touring that lay ahead. Now being reposted yet again, this time to Prestwick in Scotland, Bryan found himself sitting in the centre gun-turret of a Lincoln Bomber. While gazing out of the glass dome, staring into the cloudy sky, there was an abrupt thud and the plane seemed to drop. It felt like his stomach had come up into his throat. But this was his first flight, and so he just assumed that it was all part of the flying experience. As the plane lurched and rolled, he looked down and noticed that the pilot was struggling with the controls. The plane was obviously losing height rapidly, and yet Bryan still felt confident because he was 'in the hands of the professionals'.

Bryan was reflecting that this flight felt rather like the holiday roller-coaster ride that he had experienced as a child, when suddenly the plane seemed to right itself. It levelled out, and he could see the airfield in the distance. As the craft sped along the runway, he could sense the relief among the crew, but it wasn't until the engines had stopped and the pilot had turned round that the seriousness of the situation suddenly dawned on him. The pilot's face was green, and he explained that they had hit a gigantic air pocket over Lincolnshire which in seconds had caused the aircraft to plummet 7,000 feet. At one point he had thought that he was not going to be able to pull out of danger in time. As he began apologizing to the crew Bryan suddenly remembered the certificate he had signed, saying that if a plane ever crashed with him on board, the RAF was not to be held responsible. Bryan abruptly started to feel sick, and was the first to hurriedly disembark from the aircraft. It was certainly a near thing, and he was a bit more cautious after that, and much more aware of what went on in aeroplanes. He says today, 'It makes me shudder when I think that my life could have ended so early.'

Arriving at Prestwick was like a breath of fresh air for Bryan. The countryside was beautiful, the camp at RAF Redbrae was set among pine trees, and Bryan loved the job. He was particularly pleased that he was based close to the sea. An older local lassie took him under her wing and invited him into her home for tea most weekends. Like a surrogate mother, she would ply Bryan with home-made cakes and sponges. The cakes and the attention were very much appreciated by Bryan, but not because the food back at the base was as dreadful as it had been in Padwick. It was all cooked by local ladies, and the airmen lived like kings, while the country at large suffered the shortages and austerity of the early post-War years. Prestwick was also still a civilian airport, and from the viewing platform of the control tower Bryan watched Stratocruisers, Constellations and other giant aircraft landing and taking off. One of his jobs was to read the air-frame numbers as the planes arrived, using a superb pair of binoculars. He had to move the binoculars fast enough to keep up with the aircraft as they landed, while reading the small numbers painted on their tails. Bryan soon became an expert in this difficult job. He was also enlisted to train the new intake – or 'sprogs', as they were called – in the intricacies of the antiquated telephone system.

Despite the excitement of working with planes, deep down inside Bryan was still depressed. He felt unhappy and awkward, and it showed. The other officers were understanding. Adjutant Pilot Officer Fry had noticed Bryan's discomfort and, knowing what would cheer the young man up, took him under his wing and introduced him to the local amateur dramatic company in nearby Ayr.

'My first play with the local players was *The Ghost Train*, with me making all the train noises. The queen bee there was a lady who was famous for being on advertising posters before the War. She lived in some elegance in a fine house in Ayr, where we rehearsed. One day she invited me to an "evening" at her house. Full evening dress was required, which I didn't have, so I turned up in my brightly buttoned RAF uniform. A distinguished gentleman asked me how life at Prestwick was, and I told him it was splendid. On the way back to base I was told by the adjutant that I had been talking to Sir Basil Embray, our Air Commanding Officer! Later on he visited our base at Leuchars, and I gave his car my best salute as he was driven past. An arm full of gold braid was raised in reply – a great moment for me!'

There was no time to settle down, though, and he was soon shuffled off to Aclington, a fighter station in Northumberland that was later to become an open prison. There Bryan encountered the excitement of jet planes – Oxfords and Harvards – as well as the odd Spitfire and Hurricane left over from the War. But his depression deepened. He was missing his part-time theatrical pursuits intensely, and the much-needed boost that it gave to his morale.

Maybe his officers felt that giving the airman more responsibility would shift these incessant 'blues', for Bryan was soon promoted, being given the job of training new recruits. It didn't seem to make much difference, though, and Bryan remained quiet and thoughtful most of the time. There was quite a lot of pressure for him to stay on as his two-year period of service neared its completion – even from a beautiful WAAF who took him to one side and asked him to consider signing on for another stint so that he could appear on a recruiting poster! Bryan was flattered, of course. 'Apparently I was a bonny-looking lad who would have fitted the image they were trying to portray. Anyway, I decided against it, even though they offered the possibility of a commission, so we'll never know what might have happened.' By this time Bryan's mind was fixed firmly on the course ahead.

Sitting on his bunk one day as the incoming mail was being passed around, he was very disturbed to receive a letter from his mother saying that she was to re-marry. He was angry, as his father had only died 18 months before. Bryan was so shocked by this news of re-marriage that to this day he cannot remember whether he attended the wedding ceremony or not! He immediately drew a veil across the new life that his mother was about to embark upon, and he refused to be involved.

After the registry office wedding his mother moved out of the family home so that Bryan's grandparents could move in. Agnes and her new husband Bill lived in a house which Bryan was loath to visit. He did not like Bill, felt the marriage was too soon after the death of his father, and could not accept Bill as any kind of step-father, because 'He just wasn't my Dad!' The marriage relationship never seemed very happy, and Bryan avoided his step-father as much as possible.

Now all the ties of home life were finally cut, and he could really concentrate on the search for the one career that had eluded him so far. He wrote to Alexander Patterson, the editor of the local paper in St Andrews, Scotland. He was also a founder member of a famous theatre company of the day called the Byre. Bryan asked him for an audition for what he thought was just an amateur drama club. He was invited to Mr Patterson's house in the Lade Braes, and after a short discussion Bryan was offered the part of an old Russian Commissar in *Squaring the Circle*. Mr Patterson must have been convinced of Bryan's acting ability, as he was only 19.

Bryan found that the rest of the cast at the Byre made him feel very welcome, and when he was not in the control tower he would be found rehearsing and performing several different plays in the evenings and at weekends. Raymond and Jane Lindon were managing the Byre Theatre at the time and were the first people to pay Bryan a wage for performing. 'He earned every penny, of course,' they recall, 'particularly when cast as the Butler in *The Importance of Being Earnest*. He had to mime laying a table in time to the music from an off-stage piano which was really a tape recorder. He was an absolute knockout at this and gave the impression of having been a butler all his life.'

With his superb comic timing and attention to detail, Bryan could squeeze every last ounce of laughter and applause from an audience. Having enjoyed himself so much, he felt slightly guilty when, at the end of the first week, he was presented with a wage of 30 shillings. These were his first earnings in the theatre – and incidentally, they were more than he got for defending the realm! He also found out that the Byre sponsored a small group of professional actors. Alex was a friend who was not only kind but also very encouraging and, thanks to him, Bryan finally had a chance to get on his way towards becoming an actor.

Spending every spare moment at the Byre and playing many different roles (including Banquo in *Macbeth*, which remains very firmly in Bryan's memory as an exciting production), Bryan had found at last the fulfilment that he had been searching for. His Commanding Officer, Group Captain Robinson, had even been to see Bryan perform in *Macbeth* and several other productions, and was so impressed that he allowed Bryan more time off for important rehearsals and performances. When his two-year stint in the service was finally up, the CO called Bryan into his office and asked him what his future plans were. Though hoping that Bryan would agree to stay on in the RAF, he was not surprised when he received a straight and immediate answer from the young airman.

'I'm going to be an actor, Sir.'

'Oh yes, I've seen you act in *The Importance of Being Earnest*,' came the stiff reply. 'Carry on the good work!'

'Thank you, Sir. I'm very grateful to you!'

Bryan walked out of the dark office and into the sunshine.

5

An Actor's Life

'Show him how it's done.'
Oliver Hardy in the film Men o' War

On 15 December 1951, exactly two years after joining the RAF, Bryan was 'de-mobbed'. The hunt for a drama school had begun almost as soon as the idea of imminent freedom had entered Bryan's mind. Applying to the Northern Civic Theatre School in Bradford, he went for an interview and audition with the Principal, the intimidating Miss Esme Church. Esme was well known in the profession as one of the leading drama teachers of the day, and was highly respected by all. She had helped to found the 'Young Vic' theatre but had decided to concentrate on opening her school for actors, and had a long list of patrons including Laurence Olivier and J. B. Priestley. She was also a great actress and a clever director, and was known to be firm yet generous and kind.

Approaching the red-brick Victorian terraced house that contained her office, and armed with a glowing letter of recommendation from the Byre Theatre, Bryan cautiously knocked on the door. Hearing the clear instruction to enter, he met the formidable Miss Church, who stared straight at him. In the small room, packed wall to wall with play scripts, and without exposing the extent of his nerves, Bryan made a formal greeting and went straight into his Shakespearean audition piece from *King John*, which he had rehearsed to perfection. Esme was impressed, and after a few simple questions she immediately offered Bryan a place at her school. Bryan was delighted, but tentatively explained that he had no money to pay the course fees. He held his breath in the silence as Miss Church sat down at her desk to consider the problem. After a few moments she looked up at him, smiled, and quietly said that she was prepared to offer him a scholarship. At that very moment Bryan wanted to jump for joy, but, controlling himself, he said a gracious 'Thank you', turned and left the office. Out on the street, he felt as if he had just grown two feet taller. Something inside confirmed that this was just another step forward on his life-journey.

Despite the scholarship, Bryan still had to make ends meet by taking on any small jobs he could. This was always a problem, and it continually interfered with his ability to study properly. Miss Church was very encouraging and would often help by paying him a modest sum to go out on tour with her children's theatre to miners' halls and schools. Many of the plays were new, having been especially written by playwrights of the day who admired what Esme was trying to do.

Bryan's food and lodgings were supplied for free while he was on tour, and he remembers with affection many experiences of the infamous theatrical landladies. One particular house in Birmingham was overrun with cats. Doris Seward's home was also a regular haunt of Morecambe and Wise, who would be seen regularly tripping over the moggies lying around the house. Many years later Bryan would have the opportunity to work with these great comics himself.

The landlady had been a dancer and understood the problems associated with the business, such as late nights and the need for a lie-in in the mornings. Breakfast was served up to 10 a.m. – unless the cats had eaten it first! She used to have many celebrity guests staying at her house, such as the variety performer G. H. Elliott. Whether they were at the top or the bottom of the bill, they all paid her £4 per week for food and lodgings.

At drama school a lady teacher showed Bryan the rudiments of stage techniques, such as the 'upstage leg'. An actor should always set off walking on the leg which is further away from the audience – it looks more natural that way. She taught him how to sit down, stand up, pour drinks and exit through doors without making the scenery shudder. Bryan loved these techniques, because they enabled him to make things look real, without them actually being real. For him, this was what theatre was really all about. But he often kept in mind a famous quote from Noël Coward, who once said to a pupil of his, 'My dear boy, forget about the motivation – just say the lines and don't trip over the furniture.'

Bryan loved the opportunity to dress in costumes that were as elaborate as possible and enabled him to create many different characters. This constant natural ability to change his character caused a fellow student to remark that he would never make it in the business because no one would ever know who the real Bryan Mosley was. For Bryan was always observing those around him and mimicking their vocal styles, their mannerisms, and even the way they walked. He was so adept at creating characters that people he knew would often not recognize him. 'Having kept in touch with Norma, I invited her to one of my first proper productions at the School and bumped into her on the backstage stairs before the performance. I was dressed as the Mexican character I was playing in the play she had come to see. She didn't recognize me at all and actually asked me if I had seen Bryan. I jokingly said, "Yes, I've just seen him go upstairs", and, before I could stop her, she rushed off to look for me!'

During his second year at drama school, Esme asked Bryan to perform a short season at the Royalty Theatre in Morecambe. The huge theatrical side of the Rank Organization was starting to break up, and several well-known stars were doing guest appearances up and down the country. He was thrilled to meet his first film star, Derek Bond, at Morecambe. Bryan describes Derek as 'a marvellously handsome man'. He had starred in many films, including *Nicholas Nickleby* and a film about Columbus, with Spencer Tracy. The play they were doing together was *Busman's Honeymoon*, in which he played Lord Peter Wimsey. Robert Stephens was also in the company, along with Tom Bell and an assistant stage manager called Glenda Jackson! They were all working for peanuts, of course, but it gave Bryan the opportunity to try everything, from leading man to character acting. Although he describes many of the new plays of the day as 'rubbish', when a real 'gem' came up, it was very satisfying. Audience response was always important to Bryan, and when he played the part of a wrongly accused policeman in this production, he was delighted to earn a round of applause from the audience every night on his exit.

As he neared the end of his course at drama school, an invitation to join the religious group 'The New Pilgrim Players' arrived one day. They were to perform their biblically based plays in pubs, chapels and jails, and something inside Bryan connected. Here he could bring together the faith which he had buried since the days of the youth club, and combine it with what he loved doing best. With Esme's blessing, he instantly agreed.

It was a gloriously haphazard tour covering all of England and Wales, and visiting youth clubs, churches and even prisons.

The team of seven actors and actresses were under the direction of Pamela Keily, whom Bryan remembers as someone who lived out her Christian beliefs. An Irish aristocrat, she was tall and stately, and invariably wore a tweed cape and hat rather like those that Basil Rathbone wore in the 'Sherlock Holmes' films. Bryan observed that she made a tiny adjustment to a non-existent necklace whenever the acting company ate together. Eventually it dawned on him that she was making the sign of the cross, as if saying grace, and this moved him deeply. Pamela was also a natural joker with a great sense of humour which matched Bryan's. On one occasion she took her troupe to lunch at a convent. At the end of the meal Bryan was very amused to hear her shout, 'Right, on to the next orgy!' They all looked terribly shocked, until they saw that the Mother Superior was smiling, and with the tension released, they all fell about laughing.

The relaxed joviality must have been carried on to the performance that night, when Bryan was put in charge of the incidental music for the play. This was provided by a pana-trome – an old electric record player – attached to a pair of large speakers. Pivotal to the story-line was a scene in which one of the characters showed his expertise as a dancer. At the given moment Bryan carefully lined up the record and let it spin into action right on cue. The music blasted out of the speakers perfectly, but at the wrong speed. As the notes screeched out at a rapidly increasing rate, the poor thespian on stage gave the performance of his life, trying to keep up with the tempo! Arms, legs and torso moved in a seemingly haphazard fashion, and continued to do so even after Bryan discovered the lever which slowed everything down. The exhausted dancer, now totally confused, swung from one side of the stage to the other like a demented ballerina. For once,

Bryan was not the most popular of travelling companions that evening as they packed the gear away and set off for another destination!

They journeyed from one side of the country and back again in an old van that was kept going by prayer-power. Eventually it broke down and was replaced by an old Dennis bus given by some supporters of the group in Bristol. This tour, although one of the most chaotic jobs of his career, was a wonderful experience for Bryan and caused him to reflect once more on his own faith. His Christianity had always been very much in the background. His belief in God was very deep, but until now it had had no real relevance to his everyday life. 'I spent some time considering where I was with God, particularly as I lived at Durham Cathedral in the Bishop's Palace for a while. My short talks with the Bishop made me realize that I must take my faith more seriously, and I began to read my Bible on a more regular basis. I even began to consider for a time whether I should become a missionary.' This reflects the concern that Bryan has always had for others. He revelled in opportunities to help people to improve themselves, and was never heard to put anyone else down.

During one particular Bible study some words from Ephesians 4 jumped off the page at him: 'Do not continue to live like the heathen … Instead be kind to one another, and forgive one another, as God has forgiven you.' Bryan recalls, 'Really the whole of this passage had a profound effect on my life at that time. Of course, it still does, because, amazingly enough, unlike any other book I know, the Bible is never out of date. The language that the Bible has been translated into may have changed over the years, but fundamentally the message remains the same. I was determined to make sure that my faith remained an essential part of my life and career in the theatre from that moment on.

'I realized that God is never out of date either. He lives outside of time, and is not restricted like I was. More importantly, he understood exactly where I was at that moment and how I was feeling – better than I knew myself, in fact. Because he understood me so well, I knew that he could bring me comfort when I was hurting, confidence when I was low, and calmness when I was worried – which was most of the time! As I struggled with thoughts about whether I would ever actually make it in the profession, it was so important to me that God would always be by my side. Whichever way my future went, whether I ended up working in a shop or became a big star, I knew that he would be there for me. I was determined that I would be there for him too.'

Completing a three-year stint at drama school meant that the fun was over and the more serious hunt for an agent and an Equity card had to begin. One of the frustrating things about trying to get into showbusiness is the age-old problem of not being able to get your first job without an Equity card, and not being able to join Equity without a job. Bryan, however, was again one step ahead of the other students, having already acquired his union card during his time at the Byre Theatre, where two professional actors had sponsored his application. Bryan was eventually to become an honorary member of Equity, which meant that his membership would be free.

Getting an agent was another difficult hurdle for Bryan to overcome. The main reason for this was that most agents refused to put Bryan on their books until they had been to see him perform. The hardest thing was trying to persuade an agent to come and see you in the first place, particularly if you were still battling with the problem of not getting work without an Equity card. It was a very discouraging vicious circle that turned many applicants away from the profession.

It was a cruel form of natural selection which excluded from the business all those except the most determined, as it was these who would usually succeed.

However, Bryan was extremely determined to see the doors swing open in front of him. His first attempt at writing to an agent opened the possibility of representation straight away. Mrs E. V. M. Mullings, otherwise known as 'Mrs M.', was so impressed with his single-minded ambition to be an actor that she accepted him on the spot, and was to have Bryan on her books for more than 30 years. An incessant chain-smoker, she was never seen without a hat, and Bryan wondered if she even wore it in bed. A very kindly lady, full of advice for young actors of the day, she was also renowned for her honesty. Although she did persuade directors and casting agents that Bryan was worth considering, Mrs M. was not what Bryan called a 'go-getter'. This was to frustrate him enormously, and he felt that there were many opportunities that he missed because of this.

Still, Mrs M. cared a lot for Bryan, and pushed as much work his way as she could. She was to supply him with all kinds of opportunities, including a part in a West-End play which he never took up, feeling that it was not right for him. Ironically, he was never given the chance to appear in London again, but he has no real regrets over this.

In fact, it was while visiting London that he was introduced to David Steuart and Marjorie Denche, who ran the highly rated Perth Repertory Company. They liked him, and offered him his first professional role as 'Lofty' in *Seagulls over Sorento*. He was to be known as 'Lofty' by the locals ever after, no matter what role he was playing in the nine other productions that he appeared in during that season. Russell Hunter, a fellow actor in the company at the time, thought that although being called 'Lofty' might have made Bryan an obvious target for the local thugs, the tough-guy characters that he was playing in other productions probably saved him from a thorough beating.

A 1955 issue of *The Scotsman* carried the first ever professional review of Bryan's acting ability. It describes him as 'very good as a policeman'. Almost as an aside it finished with 'Also in the cast was Peter O'Toole.' The rest of the acting company were a bit miffed at having been left out of the first season's review, but Bryan was delighted. Perth also gave him the opportunity to direct his first fight scene for *Othello*. Calling on all his private instruction, drama-school teaching and street experience, Bryan took a deep breath and launched into a rather over-complicated set of moves designed to impress. 'A rather scratchy sword fight' is how Bryan describes the outcome, yet this experience was to prepare him for the more serious fights that were to come later in his career.

Bryan got a thrill from being in the theatre from the moment he stepped through the stage door. He says being an actor is both invigorating and at times terrifying. 'Getting ready in the dressing-room was a very strange time, as the make-up and the costume can transform actors into unknown people. Trying to stay "normal" between getting ready and going on was the most stressful time of all for me. The audience would either react as I hoped or become a dark, silent monster waiting to see me fall. I decided that acting was a very strange existence. The more unlike myself I became, the more remote I was towards others. I noticed how some parts took actors over in a much more vigorous way. I shared their need to unwind properly after a performance so that the character was never taken home with you. The challenge that each performance offered could be very exhilarating, but there was always a kind of depression after a show. That particular performance was now gone for ever, no matter how many times the show was repeated. Every audience was a new challenge. To be successful in a part could be oddly dangerous, as you always wondered if you could equal a great performance the next time. This was every actor's dilemma, of course. Many times I came off stage thinking how bad I was, only to be told how good I was! And when I came off feeling very smug, the other actors would sometimes ask me what on earth I thought I had been doing that night! It's all very odd.'

In the tradition of the two-weekly repertory theatres of the day, he worked tirelessly, rehearsing one play during the day while performing another at night in either Perth or nearby Kirkcaldy. This concentration of different scripts meant that it was common to get the lines you were performing mixed up with the lines you were rehearsing, and he would often rely on his fellow professionals to help him out of any difficult moments he got into. Bryan's struggle with the accuracy of his lines was to become a particular problem for him throughout the rest of his career.

Lines were not the only problem for the unwary thespian. On a stage the actor should always expect the unexpected, says Bryan. 'Collapsing chairs, bottles that won't open, guns that misfire – it all happened to me! On one occasion a gun refused to go off in a play. It was essential for one of the characters to die in order for the play to continue, so a paper-knife was picked up, but the blade fell off! In desperation the actor kicked the victim, shouting that the boot was poisoned. The wounded character obligingly collapsed in a heap, and the play continued.'

Bryan's pet hate was plays that required several costume changes, particularly rapid ones. However, he found lots of ways to speed things up, and only once made the mistake of not checking his fly zip. This must be the most classic mistake to make, but often, by the time the actor has come on stage and has realized that he is undone, it's too late. Bryan says that his fumbling around on stage, trying to suitably adjust his trousers during the scene, just drew the audience's attention to his problem even more. Kilts were tricky too, he recalls. 'Many a time I have rushed on stage in a classic play wearing the nearest blanket for a kilt. It's strange, but audiences never seem to notice. It's all "kidology", after all.'

Armour is one particular type of costume that Bryan is particularly wary of. This is all due to an embarrassing moment on stage during a tatty production of *Joan of Arc*, when the metal suit he was wearing caused some serious technical problems. Saying his exit line, 'It will ring throughout France. It will ring forever 'till France is free!', he was astounded to find that he couldn't get his sword out of its sheath. He was supposed to wave it around in a gesture of defiance, so he just waved his arms around and looked as angry as he could instead. Further problems were to follow. When he then turned to exit he suddenly found that he couldn't move. The knee joint had seized up, and it had the same effect as if a foot had been nailed to the floor. Because he had not realized that armour was supposed to be regularly oiled, the whole suit had decided to seize up at the most inappropriate moment. Pinned to the spot with the rest of the cast aghast, he eventually managed to drag himself off with his right foot, while his left trailed behind in an utterly frozen position. It was reminiscent of the 'Ministry of Funny Walks' in *Monty Python*. This extraordinary performance left the audience bemused and the rest of the cast struggling to remember their next lines.

The season at Perth concluded with a tour of the Orkney and Shetland Islands. Repertory companies of the day were always concerned to reach out to their community as much as possible, even if it meant squeezing the scenery, furniture, costumes, props and actors onto tiny boats. Sometimes several trips across the water were needed to transport a production. Once there, Bryan had some time to admire the magnificent and rugged scenery before performing *Othello*. He also admired the performances of his fellow actors and was always eager to learn from them. He paid particular attention to the very respected actor and playwright Alan Melville. *Castle in the Air*, part of the islands tour repertoire, was one of Melville's newest compositions, and Bryan was thrilled to be playing opposite him in it.

As he began to establish relationships within the profession, it was important that his name was known and, indeed, pronounced correctly. 'It's "Mozz-ley", not "Mose-ley",' he would say. He'd been nicknamed 'Mozzo' at school, and dreamt that one day the name 'Mosley' would be lit up above a theatre somewhere.

A problem that seemed to beset the young actor was his hatred of wet, cold, windy weather. The entire season at Perth was blighted with the worst storms one could imagine. This was depressing for Bryan, but on the other hand, the audiences always increased when the weather was bad. The Orkney Islands were no better, even when Bryan used a precious day off to visit nearby Scapa Flow. The idea was to see where his cousin had drowned on his ship *The Royal Oak* when it was torpedoed by a German U-boat during the War. Torrential rain battered Bryan mercilessly as he stood on the cliff edge surveying the scene, with all those old wartime feelings surging back, making him feel quite depressed for the rest of the day.

Bryan was prone to bouts of depression which would hit him for no apparent reason and would stay with him for two or three days. Sometimes he would get up in the morning and feel down. Unable to change his mood, he would just acknowledge the fact that this was how he felt today, so he had better just accept it and get on with life. It was on such a day as this that he got a telephone call from his grandmother to say that his mother had been taken into hospital. Unknown to him, his mother had already contracted cancer before she remarried. Feelings of guilt now enveloped Bryan as he recalled how he had shut Bill out. He earnestly wished that he had known how ill she had been at the time of the wedding and had been more understanding. It was a deep sadness to him that he never really got close to his mother until she was dying. He began to reproach himself for the way in which he had handled things.

Rushing to the hospital in Leeds, he saw Agnes lying motionless in the bed. He did not realize that this was the last time that he would see her alive. Unable to do anything but wait, he was sent home without any indication of what was going to happen. Sitting alone in the old family house, he was told only a few hours later that his Mum had passed away. He felt totally alone.

His anger about his mother's re-marriage was mixed with his grief that he had now lost his only parent. A type of emotional 'shut-out' mechanism now took over. This has tended to happen to Bryan when things get tough and there are no easy answers. Consequently he has little memory of the funeral, but remembers that he never saw Bill again.

He returned to his life in the theatre, determined to use this shut-out mechanism to bury the painful past and to prove that his acting skills would soon be properly appreciated. He had also been told by an actor friend that he had a congenital problem with his voice. Apparently his vocal chords had not formed properly, and this would make him sound somewhat wheezy and husky. An actor can often turn physical defects to his advantage, and Bryan now focused on the portrayal of character leads, rather than romantic ones. He also developed a love of accents and would practise different ones for hours while walking down the street or sitting on a bus, with the result that the whole carriage would end up staring at him in great surprise.

Calling in to the Leeds Repertory Theatre one day, looking for work, he met the Director, Leslie Storm, who asked him to return two days later. Bryan knew that a hungry and persistent actor would often be put off by a producer, who would ask him to come back later, when the producer would be inexplicably unavailable. On this occasion the producer was there, and he introduced Bryan to Harry Hanson. Having been a fan of his 'Court Players' ever since his schooldays, Bryan was very pleased when Mr Hanson suddenly asked him to join his company.

It was based at the superb but sadly decaying Prince's Theatre in Bradford. Performing there twice nightly meant rehearsing one play all day, and doing two shows every night, with only Sunday to learn the next play. In the first week Bryan played an aggressive lead in *Ask your Dad*, and in the second week he played another grotesque character. Then he was told that he could play Maxim de Winter in Daphne de Maurier's *Rebecca*. Bryan was thrilled, and asked for more money. But just at that time the ceiling fell in at the theatre, so any wage rises were stopped!

Performances were suspended too, and Bryan, not one to be idle, managed to get an invitation to join the Theatre Royal Company in York. When he told Mr Hanson that he was leaving, he said in a very non-plussed way, 'That's called being in demand, dear boy. Good luck!'

Bryan's season at York in 1957 was to bring him together with a cast of actors who were later to become household names. Working under the direction of Donald Bodley were Tom Baker, James Beck, Simone Oates, June Barry, Trevor Bannister and David Burke. Bryan recalls that Donald was a very difficult man to work for, but produced such brilliant productions that the cast always forgot how demanding he was.

While in York Bryan met Judi Dench (later a Dame) for the first time when playing in the famous Mystery Plays. They were earning £18 per week, and since the national average wage was £10, they were doing very well. As the Virgin Mary, Judi played alongside Bryan's excellently repulsive thief, Barabbas. During a break in rehearsals one day, Bryan and Judi decided to sit in the sunshine and eat lunch together. Passers-by could not believe their eyes when they saw the Virgin Mary and Barabbas sitting side by side on a tombstone, eating fish and chips!

The Queen and Prince Philip came to see the open-air drama in the street, as it would have been done hundreds of years ago, when the first recorded script is of Mary visiting the empty tomb. Regrettably, Bryan's old thorn in the flesh, bad weather, caused the performance to be cancelled. They met the Queen and Prince Philip in a local barn, but somehow it wasn't the same. It was to be some 20 years before Bryan would meet his Sovereign again, still in the open air, but on a quite different street.

It seemed that a future of playing absolute villains was already being carved out for Bryan. For not only was he playing Barabbas, but also Malchus, the accuser of the apostle Peter, and Belial, a hideously foul junior devil. Bryan relished these parts and spent a lot of time alone preparing himself before a performance took place. He believed that his Christianity gave him the best chance of portraying dark characters, because his faith gave him a greater understanding of what the darkness of the human soul was all about. He could, as it were, view good and evil from a distance and see the distinction. The play was also an opportunity to consider his own faith once more, almost as if God was bringing him to a place of spiritual re-examination. He acknowledged that he really did have a sense of needing to grow in his faith, and found that God's presence while he was playing Barabbas was quite extraordinary. He found it fascinating to take a look at a core part of his faith from a different angle. Not from the point of view of a supporter, but defiantly, from the opposition! Some reports had said that Barabbas was so amazed at being released in the place of this good man Jesus, that he actually became a follower of Christ himself. Bryan likes to believe this is true.

There were many instances where Bryan claims that he felt the hand of God on his life in very practical ways. At this time he was rehearsing in York during the day and playing in Harrogate in the evening. 'It was a play called *Worm's Eye View*. Leaving the rehearsal room later than I should have, I missed the bus to take me back to the theatre. It was thick fog, the roads were deserted and I suddenly panicked, as I knew there was no way I was going to get there in time. I started to pray, and suddenly a car pulled up. I was amazed when the driver leaned across to the passenger window and asked if I needed any help. Explaining that I needed to go to Harrogate, I was astounded when he told me he was one of the directors of the Little Theatre in Ipswich, and that he understood my problem and would drive me to Harrogate. I got there with time to spare, and reflected on how God cares about even the everyday, mundane situations we come across.'

With the season at York over, and with the prospect of another gap of unemployment stretching out before him, Bryan turned to another source of comfort and relaxation. He had never abandoned his love of painting and drawing since his days at art college. Sitting at the top of a deserted hill or in the middle of the Yorkshire Moors, Bryan would be found dabbling with his sketchpad and pencil, while dreams of having his own exhibition one day sustained him during these bleak times of unemployment.

His artistry was not confined to pen and paper, however. He was just as creative when it came to theatrical make-up, relishing the fun to be had with special effects. In the days before sophisticated latex systems were developed, an actor had to rely on his own abilities to do the best he could. One of Bryan's tricks was to apply a layer of sticky spirit gum to his face. He would then take a thin sliver of rubber, cutting it into a rectangular shape and pressing it into the adhesive, stretching it out as he did so. As the gum eventually dried, it would pull the rubber into a line of wrinkles which could make a very effective scar.

Meanwhile, the arrival of television had attracted Bryan's interest. A local agent suggested that he should try his luck as a television extra. This seemed to Bryan to be the most obvious way of getting your foot in the door of this new media. 'I did love theatre, but it was very frustrating, as I just wasn't getting the parts I should have got. Everybody seemed to be jostling for the roles I wanted and beating me. Even though I was doing great shows like *Charlie's Aunt* at Scarborough, working with people like Tom Baker, and getting great notices, my confidence was still low. The constant rejection in the theatre and the lack of work slowly robbed me of my self-esteem, and I really began to believe that I was no good. My agent tried to help by telling me that in one year I had been offered 34 jobs. The problem was that, like buses, they all seemed to come together. She said she had thought that knowing I was in demand would have cheered me up!'

What made him re-think his direction was discovering how much better paid television actors were compared with those in the theatre. The usual weekly wage for an actor in the theatre at this time was about £27, which could often be doubled working in a TV studio. Bryan had seen very little television at this time, so he didn't really know what to expect, but everyone was saying that this was the way forward for an actor, so Bryan decided to knock on some doors to see for himself.

After several weeks of writing, telephoning and making personal visits to all the agents and producers he could think of, he was exhausted and was becoming extremely disillusioned. Any openings into television seemed to be incredibly elusive, and with no other acting work on the horizon, it felt like he was knocking his head against a brick wall. He was forced to wonder if maybe his days in the business were finished. If it had not been for an encouraging word or two from Esme Church, Bryan may well have given up acting altogether. Thoughts of trying to get back into the Air Force as an air-traffic controller flashed through his mind. His family patron was St Jude, the Saint of Hopeless Causes, but he felt that maybe even a saint couldn't help him now. He was very despondent and, turning to the God whom he felt was still at his side, he now shouted with frustration and confusion. The answer came, but not as he had expected.

6

Marriage

Now I hold this hand once more
We're walking through another door
I wonder what each day will dawn
Yet want our love to be reborn.

Anonymous

Having recently heard that his childhood sweetheart had been going out with someone else, to the extent that she had actually accepted an offer of marriage, Bryan sat in his room feeling extremely downcast. He chided himself for being so presumptuous as to suppose that Norma would automatically be there for him each time he returned from a job. And now he had lost her, snatched from under his nose.

Bryan had always been attracted to Norma, even as a child. They had met when he was just 12, when she came to the Belle Vue Methodist Church with a friend. Bryan says her hair was like 'spun gold'. The church hall had a long, steep flight of stone steps which acted as an excellent set of seats for all the youth club to sit and chat on. Following her friend Margaret up the stairs, they stopped halfway while a conversation was struck up with a handsome boy who talked enthusiastically about the art of fencing. As it was not the normal sort of topic of conversation at that time, Norma was intrigued.

They became friends from the moment they met, and Norma continued to see Bryan from time to time at the youth club when she visited her friend. She noticed how sometimes he seemed to be apart from everybody else, and she would watch him as he sat in a corner on his own, drawing with sketchpad and pencil.

Norma lived in Harehills, a suburb of Leeds, and it became a weekly ritual that Norma would make the hour-long walk across Woodhouse Moor to see her friend Margaret, joining her for any of the local youth activities at Belle Vue, and often bumping into Bryan at the same time. The young girl enjoyed the thought of seeing Bryan; they always seemed to have such interesting conversations. Sometimes they would arrange to go to the pictures as a group, and Norma noticed Bryan's fascination with the cinema and admired the knowledge he seemed to have about the world of film. While the girls laughed and giggled, Bryan was perched on the edge of his seat, glued to the screen. She found his single-mindedness attractive, and hoped that their acquaintance would continue.

Norma was totally unaware that Bryan was already making sure that she noticed him, creating moments where they would accidentally find themselves sitting next to each other, or walking together while on the way to the park with the youth club. She did not know that Bryan was gently engineering their relationship. As Bryan and Norma saw more and more of each other, their naturally developing friendship became deeper, but was still full of childhood innocence. Even when Bryan started to show his fondness towards her, occasionally looking at her in a certain way, or buying her a small gift, she still only ever thought of him as a good friend, and nothing more than that.

Much later, when they were in their teens, the youth group started pairing off, and Bryan and Norma spent a lot of time together. Even then, to Norma it was just a sincere friendship, with no emotional attachments. They confided in each other, and Norma shared with Bryan many thoughts and experiences. 'He was a very good listener, and was always available for me,' she says. 'I shared things with him that I wouldn't have talked about if I thought that our attachment was a romantic one. We discussed everything under the sun, and felt an incredible freedom in doing so. If I had seen him as a boyfriend I would have been too busy impressing him in other ways.'

Bryan's availability to Norma seemed unstoppable, as he would cancel or alter all types of engagements to be at Norma's side. She would only have to ask him to help her babysit or escort her to a particular event, and he would be there, often walking as much as six miles to meet her. Trams were sometimes available, but would not always take you where you needed to go, and in order to save pocket money and be able to spend a little more time with your loved one, walking was a good solution. For they would walk together too, and this provided an excellent opportunity for the two friends to chat for hours, debating every kind of subject.

Within Bryan this platonic relationship gradually developed into a growing and deepening love for Norma, which caused him to compare any other girl he met against the perfection he saw in her. She was his 'spirit level'. 'Norma was always at the back of my mind, and no other girl really had a chance. I loved her deeply, but it was difficult to tell her. I thought that expressing my feelings for her might push her away and even destroy the wonderful friendship we had, and I didn't have reason to believe that she felt the same way towards me.' For the time being he was content to enjoy the meeting of their lives without the meeting of their hearts.

This was not to say that Bryan did not hope that he would one day win her over completely, but at this stage of his life there was plenty of time and plenty of space to keep such decisions for another day. There was also the time to experiment with other relationships. Bryan often took other girls to his beloved cinema. There were also other palaces of fun, such as the local roller-skating rink. He nervously asked one of his first girls to join him for an evening on the track, and she accepted. It wasn't until they arrived that he discovered that she was an amateur world-champion roller-skater. She sped off, leaving Bryan to fall over, and the pair hardly met for the rest of the evening. They never went out together again.

Ruth, a beautifully proportioned red-haired girl, also accepted an invitation from Bryan. This time it was to play tennis. His eagerness to attract the girls failed even here, as she thrashed him mercilessly. After this he stuck to walking, although he did ask one girl to go pot-holing with him. She refused!

In his adolescent years, finding Norma increasingly attractive, he was often tempted to grab a kiss, or to make some advances to express his love for her. What held him back was the thought that he might actually scare her off, and that anything physical would spoil their friendship. Sex before marriage was totally out of the question anyway.

Bryan's introduction to the facts of life had come in the form of a book that his Scout leader Eddie Reynolds had shown to his parents for their approval, before passing it on to the young Bryan. Sitting alone, Bryan read how sex was not really for enjoyment but for procreation in a secure relationship. It all seemed very bland and unexciting, yet Bryan's own feelings told him a different story. Three-dimensional photographs of Diana Dors, a beautiful actress and model in an enticing yet fully clothed pose, were the most erotic pictures he and his friends would see. Yet the worry of something that felt dangerous kept most young men from experimenting in those days.

'The fear of making a girl pregnant was always in the back of our minds when courting a girl. Events behind the bicycle shed certainly took place, but these were seen as unfortunate situations to get into. The local fish and chip man's daughter had a boyfriend, and she became pregnant. The stigma attached to that forced them to get married even though they had no real feelings for each other. They were the subject of much local gossip for months to come. We all felt very sorry for them.'

'Contraception was never talked about, and when the barber asked me if I wanted "Anything for the weekend, Sir?" I thought he was offering me some Brylcream, so I politely declined. A friend of mine went into a chemist to get some rubber gloves for his mother. The lady behind the counter, used to embarrassed young men asking for the personal product in an unwritten code, asked him what type he would like. "Durex, Sir?" "No, Dunlop," he replied.'

His first kiss with Norma at the age of 17 is permanently etched in Bryan's mind as one of his fondest memories. Walking Norma home from yet another night at the cinema, he was about to say goodnight in the normal way, when the urge to touch her became too great. Leaning forward, he gently pressed his lips against Norma's. His heart stopped when, rather than giving him the feared slap on the face, Norma responded with an embrace. He skipped back home, the happiest lad on earth.

While in the RAF, living away from home, he found that he was missing her. He had seen her whenever he had been on leave, but, realizing that he had taken her friendship for granted over the years, it was only when he could not be near her that he felt the heartaches of fondness within him. He decided that somehow he should try to restore their relationship. Then, to his wonderment, he was stationed just outside Newcastle, where Norma was at a convent training to be a teacher. His old favourite, the cinema, was always top of the list, and he was delighted that Norma was willing to accompany him to visit the big screen. The problem was that Norma had to be back at the convent college by 9 p.m. This meant that they would only see half the film. His deepening desire to see Norma was put to the test when he had to decide between her and his passion for films. He chose her. He started to visit Norma as often as he was allowed to, and one evening he asked the Mother Superior for an extension to the early curfew, as he was taking Norma to see a Shakespearean play. Having been granted permission, they left, and Bryan guided his sweetheart straight to the variety theatre, where the risqué singer and comedienne Sophie Tucker was performing. Keeping their heads low, and feeling slightly guilty, they were never discovered.

The competition he now faced came from a man who was the son of a wealthy businessman responsible for building many well-known bridges abroad. Added to the stark realization that he might lose the girl of his dreams was the fact that her proposed husband was to whisk her off imminently to South Africa. Bryan couldn't believe it and refused to accept it. Now was his only opportunity to win her back.

Bryan had started proposing to Norma when he was 21, but his advances had always been refused by the girl whom he felt was still 'the only one for me. There was no one else like Norma – she's totally unique.' For more than a year Bryan proposed to her repeatedly, cajoling and encouraging her to rethink her position. Norma could not understand why Bryan would want to marry her. She felt it would spoil the perfect friendship they had, and she told him so. It did not deter him. Bryan would raise the question every time they met. Pushing aside any emotion, he would ask the straight question, only to be answered by Norma's firm 'No!'

The Gaiety Theatre in Leeds showed all the best films of the day and had been a frequent meeting-place for Bryan and Norma. It was there (appropriately enough, during a screening of the film *The Red Badge of Courage*!) that Bryan asked once again. It was a deeply moving film and set the scene perfectly to pop the question once more. He said the usual words in a quiet but definite way, and to Bryan's amazement, Norma replied with a very nonchalant 'Mmmmmm,' which he immediately knew was a firm 'Yes.' Norma realized that he had caught her 'on the hop' somewhat. As she hadn't actually said 'No' this time, she felt that she should stick with it. A shared smile and a squeeze of hands confirmed and consecrated their decision, and the Gaiety Theatre became a memorial for their love, which was to remain steadfast for more than 40 years.

Strangely, more than 20 years later, after Bryan had become very well known, he was to receive a telephone call from a colleague at Yorkshire Television saying that despite the cinema having been demolished, he now owned one of the heads from the statues which had stood in the main entrance. Bryan asked if he wanted to sell it, and after he had recounted the story of his courting days, and that final victorious 'Yes', the man happily agreed. Bryan was thrilled, and the head now sits proudly in his front room. 'I met Norma when she was 11 and we got married when she was 24,' says Bryan. 'Some courtship, eh?'

They became unofficially engaged, and Norma carefully told her previous suitor that she had changed her mind. She never knew what happened to him after that, but somehow she didn't miss him. However, Norma's father, John, was not at all happy with the arrangement and, to Bryan's dismay, refused to agree to a union between them. Norma was his only daughter, and he wanted proof of how the young actor would be able to earn enough to keep his offspring well looked after. As a wood-machinist he was used to a steady job with an income he could rely on. How could a jobbing actor support Norma in the way that he had supported his wife? Seeing Bryan's protestations, he even offered to pay for him to be trained for some other 'decent' career, such as teaching, but he would not even entertain the thought of a life in the theatre. Bryan was hurt and rejected, and became determined to prove to John that he was wrong.

Bryan continued stubbornly to refuse the offer of retraining, even though he was getting very few theatre jobs at the time and was having to supplement his income by selling encyclopedias and working on a fruit stall in Leeds Market. Yet the confidence within him that one day he would make a proper living out of acting meant that he was not prepared to give up all that he had fought for and believed in. Many arguments later, and using all his performance skills, the future son-in-law managed to convince Norma's father that he was already the best actor around and that he would be able to support her. He just needed the right opportunity. Norma's father reluctantly agreed, and man and youth shook hands. He had won the prize! To this day he does not know how it finally happened.

Sadly, his initial efforts to prove himself able to support his new wife-to-be backfired when he went back to the repertory company at Perth and asked for a massive £2 per week rise. He quickly found himself jobless once more. On top of this, Bryan found his future parents-in-law increasingly difficult to get on with. 'John and Nora just didn't like the kind of things I liked. We really were like chalk and cheese, and I resented spending time with them. I did have respect for them, out of my love for Norma, but they could never understand what made me tick, and what my chosen profession really meant to me. Even later, when I was regularly appearing on the TV screen, they could not accept that I had a "proper" profession. I would treat them to expensive presents and holidays, but they were always perplexed as to where I got all the money from. I found this so frustrating.'

This family tension only served to bring the young lovers closer, and the engagement ring was duly discussed. Bryan had many years previously given Norma a gold ring which could be used to make a seal in melted wax featuring the letter 'N'. Having bought the bloodstone ring from a second-hand shop in Leeds, he felt that this was sufficient as an engagement ring too. Norma disagreed, and Bryan accepted that a proper diamond ring was the only way to assure Norma that his commitment was genuine. He saved fastidiously by working many hours of overtime and, with the money in his pocket, they went down to the local jeweller to chose the item of Norma's dreams.

It was years later that this engagement ring proved to have even greater significance, as it was pawned constantly in an attempt to survive financially. In fact the ring was pawned so often that Norma stopped wearing it, feeling that it belonged more to the pawn shop than to her. Discovering it one day at the bottom of her drawer, she decided to wear it once more. She was heart-broken to discover, on the way back from a shopping trip that same day, that it was missing, having silently dropped off her finger.

They remained engaged for nearly four years and sensed their love and companionship grow, without the need to sleep together. Sex, they believed, was sacred, and could wait to be explored and enjoyed within the context of their forthcoming marriage.

On the eve of the great day, Norma's family sat around sewing, in preparation for the wedding. While those last-minute hems were put up and flowers were pinned onto head-dresses, Bryan was to be found in his favourite place of comfort and security, the cinema. *Carousel* was the film he escaped into, having already played the part of Billy in the stage play. The newlywed Billy Bigelow, unemployed, bored and having to live off his wife's cousin Nettie, was a character that Bryan could easily relate to at this time. Unlike the character, however, Bryan would not consider stealing money to support himself and his future wife. He would save and spend carefully.

As was his custom, Bryan would sit while the film credits rolled and was always the last to leave the cinema. He then met his friends, including his old swashbuckling pal, David Poole, who was to be his best man. They all went to the local hostelry to celebrate his last night as a bachelor. 'We didn't get drunk, though,' says Bryan. 'Probably because, despite having saved a little money, nobody could really afford to!'

The wedding day in the summer of 1956 became a glorious affair. St Augustine's Church in Harehills Lane, Leeds, hosted the event, but Bryan was at first beset with worries that Norma might not turn up, maybe having changed her mind at the last moment. This was in fact exactly what Norma was facing. Her father wanted to make sure that she was absolutely certain, and said that even at this late stage she needn't go through with the marriage. He would do all the explaining to the waiting congregation, and she could just go away until all the fuss had died down. This kindly meant offer made Norma realize just how firm her love and commitment to Bryan really were. After she had explained all this to her father, he happily agreed to escort her to the church.

Norma was finally sewn into her wedding dress with all the family fussing around her. Once they were outside in the sunny street, a little girl from next door presented the bride-to-be with a lucky horseshoe. Norma's love of children shone through as she picked up the tot and, holding her tightly in her arms, smiled for a waiting photographer. The girl's mother was worried that this picture of the bride holding a baby might give the wrong idea to later viewers of the Wedding Album!

So on 25 July 1956 the old Irish priest, Father O'Flaherty, stood in front of the altar and, smiling, joined them officially as man and wife. The priest had earlier expressed his own concerns about the marriage, but years later was to remark to Norma on his death-bed that 'You got a good husband there, gal!' Now, as they stood together at the altar, Bryan gave quick sideways glances to the eyes of his bride as he said the lines that were to change his life for ever. He neither stumbled nor dried up. In fact both took their marriage promises very seriously in the belief that God was not only present at the wedding, but that he had actually brought them together in the first place. For them, for ever meant for ever.

The reception, held at a local hotel, was an unusually lavish affair. Norma's parents, though very humble people, had saved hard for several years to make sure that their daughter was given the best send-off. It was an extremely traditional affair, and a bus carried family and friends who were without their own cars from the church to the reception. It seemed that the day itself belonged to Norma's mother, who had allowed Bryan and Norma to invite a few friends of their own, while most of her own acquaintances seemed to be present. Bryan was uncomfortable in these surroundings and, feeling somewhat isolated, was eager to see the day end.

When Norma and Bryan were ready to leave, a taxi took them to the railway station, where they caught a train to York. A bus from York took them on to the banks of the River Ouse, which runs from Selby and continues right through the ancient city of York. It was a pretty, picturesque scene, and there they collapsed with exhaustion into an old boat which was to be their honeymoon home for the next week. Having not eaten anything at their wedding, they immediately set about looking for a place to eat. The local public house was fully booked, the shops were closed, and they ended up going to bed on their wedding night very hungry. Hunger was no deterrent, however, for the passion that exploded between them that night, having restrained themselves physically for so long. They believe that this passion, which has somehow remained with them throughout their lives together, has been an important element in keeping their relationship fresh.

Upon arrival at the river, they had been told by the boat's owners that the engine was faulty and could not be repaired. This meant that they spent the week moored in one place. One of the problems this caused was that their water supply ran out very quickly. The normal solution was to steer the boat towards one of the water fillers which was especially designed to quickly fill the tank. Without the possibility of the boat going anywhere, they had to resort to finding an old drum, filling it with water and rolling it back to the boat. It was only when they got back to their floating home that they discovered that the drum had a hole in it and that much of the water had been lost. Still, they had enough left for a kettle-full, and enjoyed a good, strong cup of tea, sitting together on the boat to nowhere.

Norma would characteristically burst out in laughter on such occasions, while Bryan would be hurt, feeling that she was laughing at him. On another occasion Bryan had stripped off and jumped into the canal for a swim while Norma watched from the side. After some moments of showing his newly-wed how good he was in the water he decided to get out, but couldn't climb back into the boat, as it tipped downwards every time he tried to haul himself aboard. Norma was immediately in hysterics, and the more so as she watched him hopelessly try to climb up the steep bank where the boat was moored. He spent some more time bobbing helplessly around in the water with Norma roaring with laughter, before the people in the next-door boat offered him the aid of a rope ladder. Bryan was furious!

On the first day of their marriage they had been determined to find a church to attend, and in the absence of any buses they were forced to hire a taxi, which drove them for miles before finding anywhere to worship. Bryan panicked at the thought of the money it was costing them, and Norma just laughed at the predicament. Nearly all of their holiday money had gone by the time they reached their destination, and any remaining pennies were duly placed in the church collection. The rest of their week was very frugal.

York Road in Leeds was the street that contained their new home. It was over the top of a grocery shop, open all hours and selling everything that the local community might need. Having arrived home at their new flat at the end of their honeymoon week completely penniless, they had to rely on Norma's parents to feed them. The shop and the flat were owned by Mr Marco, an Italian who took a keen interest in the young couple, visiting them each week to collect the £2 rent for their two-bedroomed flat.

Norma was by this time teaching in a local school. She had great compassion for several orphaned children in her class and was always telling her new husband how keen she was to adopt some of them. Bryan, as always, had an eye on the purse-strings and told Norma that it would be impossible to afford. She was never able to persuade him otherwise. The thought of having their own children had only been briefly discussed before their marriage, when Norma suddenly announced that she wanted to have six children. She beamed while Bryan totted up the cost of sextuplets in his mind.

Norma discovered that she was pregnant within the first few months of their marriage. Much to Bryan's embarrassment, the sudden arrival of a child caused many of those around them to suspiciously count the months between marriage and expectancy on their fingers. Norma's mother was going to be the main hurdle, so they decided to take the pressure off by taking her to Bryan's favourite place of comfort, the pictures. They watched the film together before Norma broke the news, but her mother was so shocked that she stormed off in disgust.

The advertisement for their flat had specifically said 'no children', and Norma made every effort to hold in her growing stomach every time Mr Marco came to collect the rent. Working for the local corporation entitled her to apply for a mortgage, which enabled them to make an offer on a terraced house in Crossgates, 20 minutes' walk away from Norma's mum.

Knowing that they could not conceal the facts any longer, they finally informed Mr Marco that they would have to give notice on the flat, as they were expecting a child. His face fell, and they were later to discover that, knowing all along about the pregnancy, he had arranged for some rebuilding to take place to enable a pram to be taken up the stairs, so that they could have stayed.

As it was, the pressure to find somewhere alternative to live led them to Crossgates in Leeds, to what they considered the perfect house – a very large red-bricked terraced property with a huge back garden. The price of their new four-bedroomed home was £1,200, but a friendly solicitor had convinced the owner to drop the price by £100 – the amount that the young first-time buyers were short of. Their mortgage cost them £6 a month and, as they exchanged contracts, Bryan knew that the pressure would be on him more than ever to make sure that the money was found.

Jacqueline was born on 1 May 1957, just ten months after their wedding. Bryan went with Norma to the hospital, but in the culture of the day, he was not allowed to be present at the birth. He had not expected this, but was not unduly upset. He simply arranged to get the night bus back home, and would have made the journey quite happily had he not been stopped by a suspicious policeman on the way. Asking to search Bryan's holdall, his curiosity was aroused by the contents, which included several items of women's clothing. The policeman gave Bryan a very strange look, but he eventually believed his story that he was bringing his wife's clothing back home from the hospital. With an air of slight amusement, the policeman finally sent him on his way. Bryan and Norma found that they were 'natural' parents with a great fondness for tiny feet, and they settled into their new role and their new home admirably.

Their new street was a dramatic and colourful place. 'The fish and chip shop and the chapel were sandwiched between an abattoir at one end and a brothel at the other,' recalls Bryan. 'We saw a man chase a woman along the street with an axe one evening! We had our own dentist in the street too. I remember that I had five teeth filled in one session. I couldn't talk much afterwards, but the fillings lasted for years.'

A friendly shopkeeper and a coalman would also offer the young couple goods on credit, which would often help to bridge the gaps between Bryan's elusive jobs. And their neighbours were always ready to help with practicalities such as babysitting.

In 1959 Bryan's beloved Grandma died. This was made worse by the fact that his Grandad died soon afterwards. Bryan felt deeply grateful to them for all they had done for him, and although he hadn't seen much of them in recent years, he really missed them once they were gone. Without them, there was a deep, aching gap in his life.

Theatre work was only dribbling in, but suddenly Bryan was offered a repertory season at Butlins in Clacton. This was fortunate timing for Bryan, as his second daughter, Simone, had been born a few months earlier, and a financial 'crunch' was looming once more. Clacton was a traditional seaside resort, and Bryan immediately saw the opportunity to take Norma and the two girls with him for an extended summer holiday. He was surprised to see in his contract that the management would not be offering accommodation, as he had expected. This was because they felt that actors gave the camp a bad reputation for sexual liaisons. It is ironic, of course, that the camp was already quite active in this respect, without any encouragement from the entertainment profession! Also, Bryan and Norma had already discovered that their third baby was well on the way.

While the rest of the world publicly frowned on illicit affairs and extra-marital liaisons, it was expected that members of the profession would have sexual relationships with those they were working with. This has a lot to do with the unique circumstances which surround the profession, such as long, exhausting hours, weeks away from home and the closeness which inevitably develops when working intimately with others.

For Bryan this pressure was always present, but it was his total dedication to Norma and the children which seemed to steer him clear of all the traps. His Christian faith also led him to believe that having a wrong relationship with someone else was a sin, would displease God, and ultimately would bring a lot of harm into the lives of those involved. More importantly, he did not want to do anything that might lead to him losing Norma.

Sometimes his decision to stand firm in this area caused him to be ostracized and jeered at by colleagues. He would be viewed as on oddball, but this never really seemed to bother him. None of his colleagues ever confronted him. They knew that he had been trained in the RAF to fight, complete with a short commando course, and were happy to keep their distance. He sensed that they respected him, and some were even jealous that he was able to have true freedom in this way, when in reality they did not.

Bryan was a virgin when he first met Norma and felt that trust was still an essential ingredient in their marriage. While Bryan was often away on tour, they would expect that each would be faithful. This faithfulness was to be the mainstay of their relationship in the years to come. If this trust was ever put to the test, it was only in the naive innocence that Bryan had in relationships with other women. During an earlier hunt for touring digs, one young member of the company had offered him the opportunity to share an apartment with her as they travelled around. Shirley Anne Field was one of the most attractive female members of the company, and Bryan readily accepted the invitation. Gaily telling Norma of his successful find, he was astounded when she was horrified. Despite Bryan's words of reassurance that 'nothing would ever happen', Norma was concerned about what the newspapers might say if they ever found out. She persuaded him to cancel the arrangement, but he felt that he had missed an opportunity – not an opportunity to have an extramarital affair but to save money!

The ban on actors staying at the Butlin's camp meant that the Mosleys had to find rented accommodation outside. Bryan enjoyed the early morning stroll, half a mile along the beach promenade, to work each day. It was the sort of exercise that prepares one for the difficult day ahead. It was certainly an extremely demanding schedule. He was to perform six new plays every two weeks, with up to three performances a day. Bryan relished the challenge and rose to it admirably. His love of accents and dialects was put to the test when he had to play a unique variety of characters including a vicar, a policeman, an Australian and a Scotsman, complete with bagpipes.

It was because of this season that he was to meet Derek Ware, a fellow actor. They instantly hit it off, and shared a dry sense of humour and a penchant for schoolboy pranks. Despite many differences too, a deep and lasting friendship quickly developed between them. Derek remembers meeting Bryan for the first time in a rehearsal hall somewhere in London. 'He had an unusual habit of standing beside you and looking at you out of the corner of his eye. It made you feel a little wary, like you were being spied on. He sometimes seemed aloof, but he was very encouraging to me, and I never heard him put anyone else down.'

Derek had told Bryan that he wanted to become a stunt-man. Bryan was not particularly impressed, but had always enjoyed the art of fencing since his days at drama school. They discovered a love of stage fighting, and would spend hours together honing each other's fighting skills in several of the plays that they performed together. 'We noticed that several of the chalets at the camp had huge baskets of dirty laundry sitting outside them. We got into the habit of climbing onto the roof of one of them after the show when it was quite dark, and jumping off straight into the pile of dirties. I can't imagine what anyone would have thought if they had spotted us!'

One of the plays, *Cosh Boy*, ended in a spectacular fight between them which often got a standing ovation. As the ovation became a regular occurrence, they would work hard to retain the dynamics and enthusiasm which produced this effect. 'It was quite exhausting fighting with Bryan each night, as he was such an energetic character and there were always a lot of sparks flying between us. The secret of not totally exhausting yourself lies in being able to pace your energy each time you do it, so that you have enough left for tomorrow night's performance too. Bryan seemed to be able to give just enough energy with just enough control, and he was very consistent in his fights from one night to the next. I admired him a lot for this.'

In another brawl Derek was armed with a cut-throat razor while Bryan had only a pillow. The floor very soon became covered with feathers. Bryan had to collect these up at the end of each performance, stuff them back inside the pillow, and sew it up ready for the next show.

To enhance his earnings, Bryan also took on other jobs, a practice that was actually forbidden in his acting contract. Many of these jobs took place in the evening, after the show, including working as a night-watchman, which meant that Bryan was free to share his daytimes with the family. It was a hot summer and a happy time for them all.

When they arrived home at the end of the summer, Bryan's work dried up once again. Some radio work presented itself, but it was never sufficient to reduce the agonizing worry of how the next bill would be paid. Bryan resented having to rely continually on Norma's mother to bail them out when times were hard. Though always showing kindness, Nora continued to belittle her son-in-law. Her obvious disappointment about Bryan's inability to earn a proper and consistent wage to support his family only enhanced his own feelings of resentment and insecurity towards her. Norma would do supply teaching for a local headmistress when Bryan was out of work for any length of time, but in the eyes of most people of the day any husband would be failing in his duty by having to rely on his wife to support them financially.

Most of the tension in their marriage was caused by the atmosphere of constant disapproval which enveloped them every time they visited Nora. She would tell them how her friends' children were buying cars and having telephones installed in their homes. She was ashamed that they were not able to live up to the expectations and demands of the consumer society that was starting to develop in the early 1960s. 'The big deal was to buy the new twin-tub washing machine, after having scrubbed your clothes in the sink for years,' Bryan recalls. If he was ever really worried by this constant criticism, he never let it show, always looking optimistically to the future.

Norma was somewhat relieved that her mother was good with the children. Nora took great delight in her grandchildren, though in later years she was always worrying that they would be spoilt by their parents' increasing wealth. Bryan found her enormously frustrating. 'I'm afraid we never really clicked, probably because she saw Norma at home doing all the work while I was supposedly enjoying myself somewhere in the theatre. She never had confidence in me, so we had 40 years of hostility to cope with. In the later years she did come to live with us during her last illness, and I made my peace with her. She had a very peaceful death surrounded by all the people who loved her, including me. I look back and think that she was actually a very courageous lady. I think "indomitable" is the word I would choose.'

Their other four children were arriving at fairly regular intervals, and it was said by neighbours and friends that Bryan only ever looked really relaxed when he had a baby in his arms. 'Helen Mary followed Jacqueline and Simone, and then our sons David Johnathan Jude, Bernard James Dominic and finally Leonard Bryan. We felt quite special, as we had six children when everybody else had just two. Neighbours loved babysitting for us.'

Like many Catholic families at the time, Bryan and Norma had agreed to use the natural method of family planning, but they found that it was not altogether successful. Bryan calls it 'Vatican Roulette', and when their fifth child was born their eldest was still only five years old. Bryan admits that this particular method would have worked a lot better had they been a less passionate couple. 'After the fifth child arrived, I joked to a friend of mine, "I wonder what causes it?" He was totally stunned, and shyly started to tell me the facts of life, before I told him I was just pulling his leg!'

Not wanting to be the absent father that it's so easy to be in the acting profession, he made every effort to come home whenever he could, mostly at weekends. This could involve travelling many miles overnight, but the children would always know when he was back home, as they would wake up and find sweets under their pillows. Rushing into their parents' bedroom, they would all climb in beside him, singing the song that had become their family theme tune when they were reunited: 'Here we are, here we are, here we are again. All good pals and jolly good company!'

However, large families need large incomes to support them, and as each newcomer to the family arrived, Bryan knew that his responsibilities to earn grew as well. When unemployment brought a lack of money, Bryan would be as imaginative as he could to raise the support they needed. 'A local greengrocer and friend, Peter Byrne, took me on in his shop between jobs, and he paid me with whatever potatoes and carrots were left over at the end of the day. This would become our evening meal, with Norma using all her culinary ingenuity to feed us. We lived together in our house for 13 years, and somehow Norma made ends meet. She was such a stable rock for us all, with her unswerving faith and amazing serenity. As the Bible says, this is "worth more than rubies". I can tell you, it's true.'

Ray Astin, a fellow actor also 'resting', employed Bryan's selling talents to disperse copies of the *Encyclopaedia Britannica*, but while Bryan tried to look forward with hope, Norma often had feelings of anxiety and frustration. 'We always felt that God would look after us, provided we tried to do what was right. But often it was hellishly hard. At times I stood at the sink crying my eyes out, worrying about how we would pay the next bill. We were literally living from day to day to make ends meet, and I wondered how much longer I could go on.' She became an expert in cooking meals that would last for days. The cheapest meat was breast of lamb, which would be boiled on the Monday, cut up into a meat-and-potato pie on the Tuesday, and made into a stew for the Wednesday. What was left became Thursday's soup. Huge Yorkshire puddings filled with gravy were another of Norma's specialities.

Yet Norma never put pressure on her husband, or underlined his financial failings. She gave him the freedom to continue his battle for work, believing that he would be able to make his career pay off one day. She was prepared to wait and face the hurdles now, for what might happen in the future. Norma's strength of character and belief in her husband was one of the things that kept Bryan from sinking into depression when times were particularly bad and he would be swamped with his own self-doubts. His love for Norma was the firm foundation that he was destined to build the rest of his life on, but he was determined to see things change as far as his career was concerned. He was going to make it work.

'I finally made a secret agreement with myself: "If I haven't got anywhere in the next year, I'm giving up the business!"'

7

Television

If you let a television through the door,
life will never be the same again.
Daily Mail, *1950*

It could be said that Bryan first appeared on television when he was just eight years old – but the TV set in question was made of cardboard! A school friend, whom Bryan describes as a 'big sister', introduced him to a whole new concept far beyond his imagination. Mary Bottomley, one of the family who shared their garden toilet, told Bryan about this wonderful new box of tricks she had seen at a friend's house. She grabbed an old cardboard box, cut out a square shape at the front and plonked it over the little boy's head. 'I bet you'll be on television one day,' she said with astounding prophecy.

'The instantaneous viewing of distant objects by electrical transmissions', otherwise known as television, curiously took quite some time to make its mark in Britain. Although John Logie Baird's televisor was demonstrated in London in 1926, more than 25 years were to pass before the television age really took hold. Until that time most people, including Bryan, still relied on the wireless for news and entertainment, and, of course, the cinema. The BBC had started broadcasting a daily programme of television shows in 1929, but few people actually had TV sets on which to watch them. The first domestic TV sets were marketed by Baird himself at 26 guineas in 1930.

The first ever television serial was a comedy called *Vine Street* and was shown only in the USA in 1938. The BBC broadcast its first feature-length film, *The Student of Prague*, a German film with subtitles, that same year. Bryan saw neither of these, and would probably have remained unimpressed if he had. There were an estimated 100 sets in the United Kingdom at that time, but by the 1950s there were more than seven million. The television explosion predicted by Bryan's young friend had arrived.

Bryan's dreams of becoming a television actor were, like the evolution of the machine itself, proving slow to realize. For some reason it seemed an incredibly difficult medium to get into, and much effort on his part had produced nothing. Then he was offered an opportunity to make his first television appearance, but only as an extra. Eager to get his foot in the door, he accepted.

Actually being paid to have your hair cut was one of the first perks of a television extra enjoyed by Bryan. Being given £10 a day to stand in a crowd in the pouring rain, to stroll down a street pretending to shop, or even to sit in a café drinking tea, extra work is an art in itself. As Bryan was to discover for himself, you must constantly look interested, alert and acting, just in case the cameras are rolling.

There is a clear distinction between an extra and a walk-on. An extra is just part of a crowd, whereas a walk-on is given some specific action to follow. Every extra hopes to be given a word to say, or if you are especially lucky, a whole line. Every time you are upgraded in this way, an extra amount is added to your payment at the end of the day.

Every extra's dream is to be spotted by the Director and singled out, and many performers have begun successful film and television careers in this way. Understandably, there is often some jostling at any given time, to make sure they can be 'spotted'. Bryan was not slow to explore techniques such as chatting up the main characters, making sure you are in the front row of a crowd scene, or even sneezing just before a 'take' – all these are known methods of drawing attention to yourself. One of the best perks of the job is the free food often served by caterers from some rusty old lorry in a field or parked at the side of the road. Many a curious stare has been directed towards a group of strangely dressed citizens eating a roast dinner while sitting on a kerb in the middle of a busy high street.

Ironically, Bryan's first television performance as an extra was walking down a street in a programme called *The Widower*, part of the ABC's *Armchair Theatre* series. His whole family stayed up to watch Bryan perform on the new TV set freshly installed in Norma's mother's house. They had already seen *Hancock* and *Bill and Ben* on the tiny screen of the Bush television, but they couldn't imagine what it would be like to see Bryan on it.

When it came to it, they were extremely disappointed by the brief glimpse they got of Bryan. These were the days before you could record programmes on video tape, so Bryan's television debut performance went in a flash. They had just about noticed him when he disappeared into the side of the set. As they were watching, the whole programme was being performed live in Manchester, but after the broadcast was finished the cast could quickly run down to a special room where they could watch a recording being transmitted to other areas around the country. The conditions that the actors were working in were extremely crude, with one tiny and very cramped studio. The production offices were sited in pre-fabs and caravans. Later this site was to grow into the enormous site that Granada now commands, but the practical problems of those early days meant that a lot of talent and energy was invested in each production to bring the drama to life. Bryan sat down with his exhausted but exhilarated fellow actors in the small room at the side of the studio, still in make-up and costume, and as he watched his own first TV performance he felt no trace of disillusionment at the brevity of his appearance. He had put every possible ounce of effort into his debut. He was quietly pleased and was sure that this was going to be the start of a new career.

In fact Bryan proved to be such good 'value' as an extra that over the next few months he became somewhat in demand among the producers of many of the early television shows. He would be asked for by name, and eventually opportunities to be more involved in particular scenes became more frequent. He was seen as professional, confident and, most important of all, reliable.

Most television programmes of the day were performed and transmitted live. This caused much panic and consternation among the cast and crew, who often worked in extremely difficult situations in order to make the drama look as realistic as possible. Bryan really didn't know how he would survive the pressure of live TV drama, but the fact that he was so dependable under stress made him an easy person to work with. It was nerve-racking to know that so many people were watching your every move, with any mistake being difficult to cover up, but Bryan had the ability to keep his stress level under control in any given circumstance.

On one occasion one of the main actors actually died of a heart attack in the middle of a live television programme! Bryan watched as one minute the unfortunate actor was saying his line, and the next he was on the floor, with a stunned silence in the studio and control room. The cast quickly worked out how to continue, and so the drama *Underground* became one of the most ad-libbed broadcasts in television history.

The rehearsal week for a TV play would consist of many runs of the different scenes, rehearsed in no particular order, and this could be a huge pitfall for the actors. On the day of the transmission, a technical rehearsal would be followed by the Director's run, before performing it live. Bryan would have moments of absolute terror when having done so many runs confused him into wondering if he was repeating scenes that had already been done.

Always suffering from extreme bouts of nervousness during these programmes, Bryan somehow kept his nerves hidden, probably for fear of being rejected by the programme makers. However, his nerves and the exhausting schedules would never stop him from falling asleep in a chair during the long periods of waiting which usually accompanied television acting work. It was during a live transmission of ITV's *Emergency Ward 10* in 1964 that Tom Adams, starring as one of the doctors, discovered Bryan's problem. 'He was playing a very nervous patient who was awaiting an operation. I was standing by the side of the set waiting for the floor manager to give me the go-ahead to start the scene, which was being watched live by ten million viewers. I rushed in to calm down and reassure this very nervous patient – and there was Bryan Mosley, in bed, fast asleep!'

On another occasion there seemed to be a fault with the sound during the rehearsals of a television version of *Coriolanus*. A groaning and grunting noise was being picked up by the microphones. The floor was covered in 'dead' bodies at the end of a battle. It was eventually discovered that one of these bodies was snoring! Bryan had exhausted himself and was enjoying the opportunity to take it easy for a few moments.

Joining his long-time friend Derek Ware for an episode of *Dr Who*, Bryan played the part of a Spanish pirate. This was in the days of William Hartnell, the first and probably best-loved Doctor. Derek remembers how much Bryan would revel in the chance to dress up. 'He was going into all the other dressing-rooms at the BBC, looking for other bits of costume he could borrow. He actually asked other actors whether they wanted particular bits of their costume and, if not, could he have them? He ended up looking like the grand captain of all Spaniards, with an eye patch and huge puffed-up sleeves. The leading performer jokingly said that Bryan looked better dressed than he did!'

As Derek had his own small flat near Marble Arch in London, he would often offer it as a place for Bryan to stay whenever he was auditioning or working in town. Derek mentions that Bryan's family would 'take precedence over everything else he did – he was a very dedicated father. With such a big family now, he was always under an enormous amount of pressure to manage his money properly, and spent as little as he could. So he would frequently hitch-hike his way down from Leeds to London and then hitch-hike his way back home afterwards.'

For one of these trips, Bryan had pawned his cufflinks in Hampstead to raise the cash for the tube fare to Derek's flat. There was a different type of 'pawn' on hand in London, as Bryan discovered when he visited his old friend who happened to live in Soho. This was a pretty heady part of town, even in those days. Bryan would describe the area as 'hot and cold running birds everywhere'. Temptations were many, but somehow Bryan never succumbed. His commitment to his family was a helpful source of strength and resilience in this area of his life.

Derek enjoyed the fact that he would never know when his mate would suddenly turn up. He remembers one occasion vividly. 'There was a knock at the door, and there stood Bryan with a forlorn-looking face. He had torn up some white tissue-paper into tiny pieces and put it on the shoulders of his coat to look like snow. He stood there for a moment looking abandoned and alone, without saying a word. Then suddenly trying to emulate the silent movies, he started to hum a tune and held up a postcard with words, like a caption. This was immediately followed by another and another: "Do you think you can see yourself clear to letting me stay here tonight?" read the final message before the humming stopped. "You daft nit," I said, "come inside!"

'His whole family stayed in my flat at one time when he wanted to give them the experience of seeing London. I couldn't believe it, as all eight of them crammed themselves into my little one-bedroomed flat, and when I asked how on earth they were going to cope, Bryan told me how he had worked out how each of them would fit in. The baby ended up in the bottom drawer of my dressing table! The actor Ron Moody even babysat for them one night.

'I did notice how much Bryan loved his food. Particularly Italian food, which was good because it was cheap. You could fill yourself up on pasta for just a few pennies, and it would last you all day. The only problem with Bryan staying with me was his snoring. It was so loud that I thought I could hear the windows rattling in time to it. I would do everything I could to stop it – shout at him, shake him – I even gave him my bed and slept in the next room, but nothing worked. I would always end up bleary-eyed when Bryan came to stay. He even fell asleep during a film we went to see together. I ended up sitting several rows away so that

I could hear what was being said on screen. It was always fun having Bryan to stay!'

Temporary housing was also provided by another of Bryan's friends, the stunt-man Barry Jackson. He owned a flat over the top of London's Marylebone Station, and insisted on climbing in through the outside window whenever Bryan went back with him. Bryan describes it as quite dangerous and unnecessary, 'but great fun!'

It was on one of these London trips that Bryan found himself working with Donald Pleasance and Patrick Magoohan in a TV drama called *The Greatest Man in the World*. Bryan said some spontaneous words to Mr Pleasance in the middle of a lull, and the Canadian director smiled and decided to keep it in. 'Oh, come on, Hyram!' became Bryan's first ever television words. He was pleased with himself at the way in which he had seized the moment, and particularly thrilled at the extra money he had earned on the spot.

The thrill that this new experience gave him caused a determination that his days as a walk-on were numbered. He enjoyed the feeling of having something concrete to contribute to a film, and delighted in the extra respect with which he was treated by his peers. Bryan visited his agent the next day and firmly told her that his 'extra' days were now over, and he would only consider doing 'parts' from now on. 'The others are not that good looking, they're not that talented. I can do better,' he said to himself.

Mrs Mullings was worried at this decision, not least as she was providing Bryan with extra work almost every week and was keen not to lose the 10 per cent commission that all agents are famed for. Yet Mrs M. had a bigger heart than many other agents, and was prepared to listen to Bryan's plea. His fellow artistes had laughed at his decision, however, and one made a

£5 bet with Bryan that he would get nowhere and be back as an extra in a few months' time. It's ironic that in a later TV play that Bryan was actually cast for, this same actor was there as an extra. The £5 was refused by a smiling Bryan, who agreed to drink on it instead, feeling a tinge of sadness for this man who himself was to remain an extra for the next 20 years.

While Bryan refused to do any more extra parts, the roles he was hoping for didn't materialize as quickly as he had hoped either. He harboured doubts about Mrs M., still wondering whether she was pushing him as much as she should. Bryan was never one to sit around and wait for the phone to ring, and decided to do some of his own casting 'research'. He knocked on any door he could to make sure casting directors and producers knew his name and what he could do. Fellow actors would even consider him pushy, but his justification was the mouths he had to feed back home. One technique he had was to become a member of the BBC club. This was a place where actors and performers, alongside musicians, producers and directors, would relax together. By keeping your ears alert to the gossip around you, it was easy to discover what productions were currently in the pipeline.

Chatting to those in the club and finding out what productions were currently being cast, Bryan would then telephone the office of the director, announce that he was in the BBC club at that moment and ask if he could pop along to see the director straight away. Several parts were obtained in this manner, but the biggest disappointment was when he heard about a new comedy series called *Dad's Army*. Rushing out to telephone the show's creator, Jimmy Perry, he was told that all the parts had been finalized 20 minutes earlier. This series went on to become one of the most popular programmes of all time, of course, and Bryan's career may have been very different had he finished his drink earlier in the BBC club that day.

Bryan was also disappointed at not being cast as Patrick Macnee's younger brother in ITV's *The Avengers*. Having waited weeks for the contract to arrive and turning down other work in its place, he decided to telephone the office, and was brutally told that the writer had changed his mind and the part was no longer on offer. Bryan seems quite philosophical about the times when all his hopes were dashed. 'That's the biz!' he would say to himself, and move on to the next goal.

Bryan took his acting very seriously and was often admired by his fellow actors. This affirmation by his peers was most important to him. Confined to a telephone box in a drama called *The Men From Room Thirteen*, he played a bomb-disposal expert frantically dismantling a bomb. The scene was done in one 'take', and he was immediately congratulated by the leading member of the cast, who said, 'My heart was in my mouth watching that, mate.' The bigger the star, the more fulfilling the compliment was to Bryan.

Compliments were not always that forthcoming, however. In one episode of *The Saint* Bryan found himself becoming increasingly irritated with its star, Roger Moore. 'He was very busy and obviously didn't have time to talk to other members of the cast,' he remembers. 'Anyway, although I only played the impressively named "First Sleuth", I still get repeat fees from this episode 30 years later!' Bryan was to appear in several episodes of *The Saint* but is actually quite keen to forget which ones.

For any actor, the publicity photo is a most important tool, and Bryan had several. They came in different guises and characters, but always had the same information hand-written on the back: 'Bryan Mosley. Height: 6 ft. 0 in. Weight: 15 stone.

Eyes: blue. Hair: light brown. Speciality: fencing and brawls. Agent: Mrs Mullings.' Casting director Tony Arnell, who had seen early potential in Bryan, pushed Bryan's publicity photos under the noses of many directors of the day, suggesting him for several parts. He even introduced Bryan to the big Hollywood film star, Bette Davis. It was through the conscientious efforts of Mr Arnell and producer Leonard White, whom Bryan had first met at Perth, that Bryan got his first big television break.

It came in the form of an *Armchair Theatre* special called *Little Doris*. The director was Charles Jarrott, a revered man who was known for getting productions out on time and within the meagre budgets allowed. For Bryan, this was a real breakthrough, and he put every effort into playing the burly character he had been given. Bryan was extremely pleased with the outcome of his performance in *Little Doris*, but his hopes of being finally 'discovered' slowly evaporated when the telephone remained quiet for several weeks afterwards.

Just as Bryan was starting to become depressed once more about the lack of opportunity, an offer to appear as a comic's stooge brightened him up and enabled him to stretch his artistic wings while discovering his talents as a straight man. Bryan is a great admirer of comedy, and enjoys a very dry sense of humour, but the bad experience which followed while working with Charlie Drake knocked his confidence in this area. 'It was in a series called *The Worker* where Charlie was playing the part of an odd-job man, often on the dole and always keen to try out new vocations. It had been written by Charlie and I was in a scene in a pub, but it seemed that I was getting all the laughs instead of Charlie. This is not a good thing in comedy, of course. Charlie was very displeased and it made me very unhappy. I asked the director if I could be released from the contract. He eventually agreed, but strangely, I still got paid and was billed on the credits, but I never appeared in the show.'

Determined not to be put off the idea of working with comedians and with a new taste for this other, light-hearted side to his profession, Bryan decided to pursue similar avenues for work, and instructed Mrs M. accordingly. Appearances with Jimmy Clitheroe and Harry Worth followed, but there was one comic he applauded the most. 'I always admired Michael Bentine. I wanted to work with him, so I wrote asking if there was any chance. His reply suggested that I should write to his director, Joe McGrath, which I did. So it came to pass that I was embroiled in the controlled lunacy of *It's a Square World* with Dick Emery, Frank Thornton, Joe Baker and several others. We were to film a spoof of *The Three Musketeers*. Unfortunately no one but Mr Bentine could fence, and he was very good, of course. So there we were at Twickenham Studios, with me teaching the others all the basics of fencing. Then Michael appeared and, hearing that I was the instructor, insisted that we had a bout together. He proved to be very fast, but I managed to keep up with his pace and thought of suggesting to Michael that we should do a *Cyrano de Bergerac* sketch in his show. I was so excited with my idea that I told Joe Baker, who promptly said, "Forget it – Michael has 20 new ideas a minute!" Sadly, we never fenced again, as the insurance risk was mind-boggling anyway.'

It was this same director, Joe McGrath, who was to telephone Bryan some weeks later to ask if he would be interested in doing a commercial. Bryan eagerly accepted when he was told it would be with his heroes Morecambe and Wise. He went to Bond Street to meet Eric and Ernie in the producer's office for lunch. Bryan asked the director what caused him to remember who he was, and was told that they had been throwing some junk out of the producer's office, and had seen Bryan's picture in the waste basket. They obviously thought he would make a good barman, as they were to advertise Watney's ale, with Eric and Ernie being served by Bryan. It was a whole week of hilarity watching the famous duo's careful method of rehearsing and recording, and Bryan was surprised at how precise comedy could be. He became firm friends with both of them.

One day in 1961 Bryan's agent called to ask if he would attend an audition for a TV series called *Coronation Street*. By this time Bryan had been given the old black-and-white Bush TV set previously owned by his mother-in-law, but as it would only receive BBC1, he had not seen any of the first episodes of this new kitchen-sink drama series.

'I sailed into the studio to audition in front of the director, Howard Baker, to read as a policeman. He liked my Lancashire accent and asked me to read something else.' Little did Bryan realize how much his life was to change in the next few minutes, as he was handed the script which featured a new character – a postal worker. Bryan read it almost as a natural extension of himself, and immediately felt a rapport with the character.

The director asked him to read some more before announcing that although he would really like Bryan to play the part, he felt that he was actually too young. Bryan, realizing that this was the chance he had been waiting for, refused to leave. He began to discuss the character at great length and how he would like to play him. Eventually he persuaded the director that he was actually ideal for the part and would be very comfortable playing the role. The director eventually agreed, and Alf Roberts was finally born.

8

Alf is Born

'He'd skin a flea and then sell it
a vest, would Alf Roberts.'
'Hilda Ogden'

Wearing a shirt collar that was one size too small, in order to make him look fatter than he really was, Bryan was told that the character of Alf Roberts should be a man who was the salt of the earth. Fundamentally, he should be played like a Sunday school teacher. 'I'm not sure if Alf has ever been to church, but he's a Sunday school teacher at heart,' says Bryan.

His first scene, transmitted on Valentine's Day 1961, saw him dressed in brown overalls, working hard to sort the mail for the GPO. Despite his confidence at being able to play and develop this new character, Bryan describes his initial years on the *Street* as quite simply 'totally terrifying. Great fun, but mainly totally terrifying. The main problem was that it went out live, and the audience was huge. This meant that if any mistakes were made, you did not have the chance to stop recording and start again. What was done, was done, and no going back. Added to this was the worry of losing your job, if you made too many mistakes. This is a fear that remains to this day. What helped one day was when I inadvertently heard one of the studio technicians say to his colleague, "Blimey, he can act!"'

Peter Adamson as Len Fairclough, Violet Carson as Ena Sharples, Bill Roach as Ken Barlow – these were some of the characters whom Bryan met on his first day in the studio. They were all jobbing actors who were suddenly in the limelight. Some were already feeling over-used for publicity purposes outside the studio and abused by the press, even in those early days. Others felt they were being ignored, which meant there was a lot of insecurity among the cast. Bryan says, 'We were all glad to be there and earning £50 a week, but the feeling of control over us was sometimes unbearable. We all reacted in different ways. Some were a bit starry – particularly Pat Phoenix, who seemed to perfume herself all day long. You always knew if Pat was in that day, as there was always a trail of strong perfume throughout the corridors. She went out one day to buy herself a new mink coat, but never told anyone she'd got it from C & A. She was delightfully "one-off".

'Violet Carson was an established actress who had been working for years, was totally confident in herself, and did not need to prove anything to anybody. She was the one whom I admired the most. Some of the others were pretty two-faced and hypocritical, and some were jealous of others getting the better lines, which caused much underhand gossip. There was also a lot of insecurity among the cast members, probably due to the six-month contracts they had, which meant that they felt they had to keep proving themselves to the management in order to get their contracts renewed. There was a constant power struggle going on, with lots of game-play between cast and management too. It seemed sometimes as if the management would try to keep the pay as low as possible in order to keep the cast under some sort of control.'

If there was ever a problem for Bryan with the scripts, it seemed to revolve around remembering other characters' names. At just the crucial moment, it seemed, his mind would go blank, and, fumbling for his words, panic would rise within him. Bryan was never one for giving up on a scene, and always found a way out, becoming an expert in live-television ad-libbing. On several nerve-racking occasions he thought his mistakes had ended his TV career. His script would arrive the week before his scenes were due for transmission. This meant that, as in repertory theatre, you would be learning one set of lines while performing another. There was always the danger that lines would be changed by the writers at the last minute – sometimes literally minutes before going on air, causing panic among the cast.

The cast were aware of each other's lines, of course, and would help one another out as best they could in times of emergency. Bryan made a lucky escape when, in the first meeting between Alf and the infamous Ena Sharples, he suddenly 'dried up' on live television.

> Bryan: Now look here, Mrs …? *(Bryan fumbles for her character's name.)*
> Ena: Sharples!! And don't you ever forget it!

After this scare, a particular method that Bryan employed to help him over the hurdle of his mind going 'blank' was one that was emphatically denied by Bryan himself. Yet the fact that he used this secret *modus operandi* on many occasions is supported by those in the cast who knew him best. The technique involved pausing with a small internal 'burp' or 'hiccup' half-way through a line at the crucial moment, which would give him a split second to remember where he was in the script, or to make up a quick ad-lib. Bryan would suggest it was just part of Alf's character, but it was certainly an incredibly clever way of overcoming an actor's worst nightmare, and, of course, it worked extremely well.

Whatever Bryan was doing as Alf, it was always his 100 per cent concern to make it as believable as possible. Even in the background scenes, the viewer would see Alf arrive at the Rovers, remove his pork-pie hat to the ladies and mumble his infamous but underplayed greeting to the others. Probably a trick left over from his early days of extra work, it didn't matter to Bryan whether you were in the foreground or background – you must still 'twinkle'!

A typical week on the *Street* would begin with the 'plotting' of the scripts on the Monday. This involved telling the actors where to stand, sit or walk, and which direction to face in, which only added to the burden of things to remember. One famous incident occurred when a canal scene was built in the studio to meet the storyline's demand for a bag to be thrown into the water. A fight was then to take place between Bryan and another actor, Bryan Rawlinson. Alf was a bit of a 'bruiser' in those days. The show was still being transmitted live, but Bryan Mosley could not remember the name of Bryan Rawlinson's character. The tussle between the two of them lasted much longer than expected because of this, but it just looked all the more realistic as a result.

On another occasion Bryan and a colleague were acting out a scene that supposedly took place in the front room of a flat. As they spoke their dialogue, a technician mistakenly wandered past the window. Bryan thought nothing of it, and afterwards he told his co-actor that he was making too much fuss about it. After all, it was quite feasible for someone to walk past a window, he pointed out. 'But not when it's supposed to be on the third floor!' came the reply.

As most of the actors were seasoned repertory players and were used to working as a team, it was probably this sense of togetherness that got them through. They were able to lean on one another, despite the hovering fear of betrayal. When the rubber hit the road, they would close ranks like any devoted family.

It is hard to imagine Bryan laughing uncontrollably, yet he is still occasionally prone to a fit of giggles. As anyone in the business knows, and as programmes that feature 'out-takes' clearly show, once an actor starts giggling, it is extremely difficult to stop. The trigger can be anything, from a fluffed line to a faulty prop, but whatever it is, the more the titters are suppressed, the more they build up inside. In the theatre Bryan has experienced moments when the cast laughed louder and longer than the audience. But in the TV studio, where wasted time is definitely frowned upon, a fit of the giggles can be even more uncontrollable. Bill Roach describes Bryan as 'very dangerous to my career. He is a very funny man, and I'm a terrible giggler.' Bryan explains, 'In *Coronation Street*, Bill Roach and Eileen Derbyshire are both dreadful gigglers. That's why I look so miserable most of the time. I'm trying to keep my face straight!'

Any new member of the cast is treated on their own merits, but is obviously seen as an outsider until firmly established as a regular character. Bryan is known for making every effort to reassure newcomers and to make them feel at home, but he still admits to watching closely to see if the new character works. If it does, he is pleased. If it doesn't, he expresses sadness for the actor or actress who has just lost a job. As he says, 'We've all been there.'

Over the months that followed his introduction to the soap, Bryan began to be a familiar face on the box, and enjoyed the experience of being recognized in the real streets around his home. Somehow it gave him the recognition that he had been searching for. His family started to reap the benefits too, and the extra money that was now available enabled Norma and the children to have the clothes and shoes they needed. Money was still tight, and with a family of eight, budgets were carefully tuned, but the enormous financial pressures of the past were starting to ease.

There were other benefits of having your dad on the 'box' too, as Bryan recalls. One year he was invited to attend an old folk's Christmas dinner. 'Roma Hogson was an artist that we were friends with, and she asked me to arrive at the dinner as Alf. The family were invited too, so we all piled into my rusty old Bedford van, which was the only means of transport large enough to carry us all.' Dad was well known for exhibiting his driving skills, as Simone points out. 'He hated being held up in traffic queues, so he would take any short cut he could up all the little side roads, which invariably took three times as long as it should have done. If we ever got caught on a tricky bit of narrow road we were all supposed to watch in amazement as Dad would do a fifteen-or-more-point turn. He thought that the more points he did it in, the better the driver he was.'

On their way to the Christmas dinner, and on one of Bryan's short cuts, they ran into a very heavy blizzard. He recalls: 'We were halfway across the Yorkshire Moors, and the windscreen wipers were doing their best to brush the snow away, but were obviously not coping with the weight of it, and were in danger of staggering to a halt. I could hardly see the road as I peered through holes in the white blanket in front of me. It would have been folly to turn back, and we decided to go on, praying all the way. It was faith and providence that got us there, battered but triumphant, at about 8 p.m. The kids were delighted to be up so late. Roma put us all in a large cottage known as "Merrymen". There we were greeted with a roaring fire in the iron fireplace. We could smell what turned out to be meat pies, hot soup and two enormous apple tarts from the coal oven. The beds even had hot-water bottles in them, and the children thought they were in fairyland.'

The next day they were due to attend the Christmas dinner at the Dolphin, an ancient smugglers' inn run by Mavis and Tony Straw, who had somehow smuggled all the old people there. They were absolutely astounded to see 'Alf' when Bryan entered the room in his white coat. They watched him remove it before sitting down to lunch with a long line of children on either side. They had three sittings, though Bryan could only manage two dinners, big lad though he was. Mavis did most of the cooking, and it was certainly a banquet. Bryan describes those days as 'glowing like a lantern in my memory'.

It was all symbolic of the fact that he was now on the path to the success that he had worked so hard for and believed so much would eventually happen. He had arrived and was determined to settle for nothing less. This was not to be, however, as within ten months of his contract a serious strike was threatened by the television staff. In the autumn of 1961 Bryan was confidently happy, as the *Coronation Street* management had asked him to extend his contract and stay on even as the strike loomed. His agent, Mrs M., had other ideas and made it very clear that she wanted him out of the series. She was all for the 'little man' standing up to the television Goliaths, as she put it.

The main problem with the contract that was now being offered to Bryan was a new clause that stated that, in the event of a strike, the actor would remain on the side of the management. Mrs M. deemed this immoral and unfair, and was determined that Bryan should not sign it.

Bryan was more concerned about the sudden loss of his wages than the politics of television, but he agreed to stand with his agent. She had always treated him fairly, he reasoned.

This was singularly true when it came to finance and pay. Unlike many other agents, who would hang on to their clients' money for weeks, she would send the fees to her actors as soon as she received them herself. Bryan respected her, appreciated her judgement and agreed to pull out. Mrs M. was pleased, but immediately worried about the welfare of one of her best actors, realizing that because he had refused work, it would not be possible for him to claim unemployment benefit.

The Mosleys were extremely moved when they discovered that Mrs M. had arranged to send Bryan £20 a week from her own savings to tide the family over. Bryan eventually paid this money back to her, by going back to Leeds Market and working the early morning shift, but not without the embarrassment of being a famous face selling fruit and vegetables. This was still preferable to the embarrassment of signing on at the dole office, though, he figured. It was a major shock for Bryan, Norma and the family. Thinking they would enjoy the benefits of the high television income for ever, they were unprepared for it to stop suddenly, and had made no arrangements for savings.

The television scenario was looking bleaker than ever and the whole ITV network was virtually blacked out for several weeks, with Bugs Bunny seeming to be the only artiste still willing to perform. The BBC were still transmitting and Bryan managed to get some work with them. This included an episode in the popular police series *Z-Cars*. After the seven-week strike at ATV had been settled, Bryan was offered a part in the long-running serial *Crossroads*. This enormously successful television production, recorded in Birmingham, ran for many years and was transmitted four times a week. When Bryan arrived on set he was immediately invited to a party to celebrate the show's anniversary. Piling into a bus, they were

above Bryan's street, Rosebank View, with not a rose in sight.

above A Scarborough holiday with parents James ('Jimmy') and Agnes Mosley.

left Attired in one of his modelling suits, accompanied by tailoress Aunt Mary.

In the RAF.

Wedding bells ring on 25 July 1956.

above Bryan, as Malchus, accuses Peter (York Mystery Plays, 1957). Also in the cast are Judi Dench, John Gatterel, Robert Rietty, Norman Tyrell and Brian Spink.

'What, no wages?' As Jo-Jo in *Up Jumped a Swagman* (ABPC).

Bryan's love of dressing up started young. (*Heart of Midlothian*, Byre Theatre, 1951)

With Michael
Caine in *Get
Carter*.
*(Movie Store
Collection)*

Yet another
brawl in *The
High Game*
with Ian
Hendry.

Is Ernie
paying?! The
Watney's
advert with
Morecambe
and Wise,
1967.

Bryan in full costume with Jill Hipkiss. (*Doctor's Delight*, Derby, 1954)

'On guard!'

A moment of madness when Bryan can't resist delving into the costume basket in the *Street's* rehearsal room.

Meeting the *Street*'s greatest fan, Her Majesty the Queen.
(Granada Television)

Memories of her own childhood flood back as the then Prime Minister Mrs Thatcher visits Alf's Mini Market.
(Granada Television)

above The Mayor of Weatherfield with Audrey (co-star Sue Nicholls).
(Granada Television)

The waxwork cast for the *Street*'s Blackpool exhibition.

Alf collects his OBE.
(Granada Television)

Bryan and Norma.

Bryan in his beloved garden.

taken to a hotel in nearby Stratford-on-Avon, which is an appropriate place for a bunch of thespians. They enjoyed a very sumptuous dinner, and the next morning went back to the studio to start rehearsing. It was the best and most luxurious first day on a job that Bryan had ever encountered.

The star of the series was the infamous character Meg Richardson, who ran the Crossroads Motel like the head-mistress of a secondary school. Everything was beautifully organized and in its place, only to be let down by her unreliable staff, her rebellious children and, of course, the tittle-tattling cleaner Amy Turtle. It was exactly the type of programme that you would watch with your dinner on a tray on your lap, and was one of the programmes that created the 'TV dinner' phenomenon. Bryan says, 'Noelle Dyson was definitely the star of the show, and was a very deter-mined lady, very like the Meg Richardson character she was playing. Many people found her temperament difficult to handle, but for some reason we got on well, and she invited me to sit in Meg's sitting-room in the studio. The actress Sue Nicholls was also in the show at the time, but we didn't get to chat much, as the recording schedule was so fero-cious. Later she told me that I should feel honoured, as only a few people were allowed to sit on Meg's sofa. I felt privi-leged indeed!

'A man who became a dear friend turned up one week. His name was Paul Dawkin, and I had met him some time before at Granada when I was starring in a series called *Villains*. Paul was a big, droll man – "The Unknown Genius", I called him. He was also very untidy and so Nolly (Noelle allowed me to call her this) forbade him to sit on Meg's sofa. So he lay there at her feet like a huge, obedient dog, and Nolly was delighted by his cheek. We worked together on other occasions too, but sadly, he had a strong liking for "John Barleycorn", which caused his early death. Booze has a lot to answer for.'

Playing many parts in the series over several years, Bryan's first role was that of the lecherous Spaniard, Señor Balda, kept at bay by one of the regular cast staying in his hotel in Spain. 'The fact that I nearly smashed the set up when I was thrown downstairs amused Miss Gordon no end, even though we had to do the scene again. I liked her very much, as she was very direct, and it must have broken her heart when she left some years later.'

In another storyline he was a Welsh lorry driver. While waiting around on set, he would read to stop himself getting too bored. On some days Bryan would arrive at the studio, wait all day to be called, and be told to go home again at 6 p.m., having done nothing, only to return the next day for the same thing to happen again. None of this seemed to rile Bryan, who would just shrug it off and make some remark that this is what television is like, and to expect anything else would be ridiculous.

Ironically, his 'digs' at the time were back at Doris Seward's house. Doris and her husband Percy had originally been an old comedy team. Having given up the act at the death of Music Hall, they decided to keep in touch with the business they loved so much by opening their home to the waifs and strays of showbusiness. 'I had no idea what memories I would keep from 77, Bristol Road,' says Bryan. 'So often we take for granted moments in our lives which we can never re-live. One week I was staying there and shared the house with the cast of a touring variety show called *Those were the Days*. Stars including Ella Shields, Randolph Sutton and Albert Wheelan were staying, and it was like a dream come true for me. Mealtimes were absolutely hilarious. Great people, great days…

'One day, while waiting to be called for a scene, I was reading J. B. Priestley's *Lost Empires*, and Nolly said she hadn't read it, so I gave her the book. Much later I was astonished when she sent it back in the post with a sweet note attached saying how much she had enjoyed it. Courtesy indeed from one of the country's best-loved actresses. She had a very close relationship with the comedian Larry Grayson in her latter years. I was very sad to hear of her death and shed a tear or two. The series was incredibly popular, but it saddened me when it was derided and "sent up" by people who had no idea of the sheer effort that went into recording the shows in a very short time. People still remember it with great affection. So do I.'

On the last day of filming, Bryan started to feel very unwell. With flu-like symptoms attacking him, he arrived home. Norma took one look at him, and told him to go straight to bed as she called the doctor. Dr Bickler, a friendly Jewish GP, called to see him, and immediately diagnosed hepatitis. This is a highly infectious disease for which there is no treatment, as any medication would automatically go through the liver and be destroyed by the diseased organ. The condition could make its victim experience fever, headaches, nausea and even jaundice. Severe cases can be life-threatening.

There was no other alternative than bed-rest at home or in hospital to give time for the infected liver to heal itself. The doctor decided it was better for him to be at home, and Norma realized that she would have to become an in-house nurse. Bed-rest was just what Bryan didn't want, of course. He had always been an active man, and there could be nothing more frustrating and upsetting for him than to be confined to his room. Added to this was the fear of losing parts, being forgotten by casting directors and the possibility of financial ruin. This was heightened all the more by the knowledge that this disease had no real time-scale attached to it. No one really knew how long it might take for Bryan to feel better, and it was acknowledged that the infectious period for the ailment could be several weeks. It caused Bryan acute mental depression. 'My real friends came to see me, the others steered clear,' he recalls.

Bryan's constant concern for others was expressed in the worry that he may have infected some of his colleagues. In particular, he had just been filming a scene in which he was repeatedly kissing an actress who happened to be pregnant. He wrote a letter to her husband, suggesting that he should get her tested for the disease. Fortunately the test proved negative.

Six weeks later, Bryan was still isolated in bed. Moments of depression and boredom were only broken by his children Johnathan and Bernard, who would perform songs and sketches at his bedside. It was these moments of being with his family that he feels helped pulled him through. The realization that his family meant so much gave him the hope he needed in his worst moments. 'I told myself I was not allowed to die, I must get better.'

Norma remembers that it was often a familiar pattern that Bryan would work extremely hard, going from job to job and from one part to another, until the work dried up and he would collapse with some illness. 'It would be a cold or an infected throat or whatever, as if he was catching up on the illnesses he was due to have. Then he would just get himself better before work would come in again.' This pattern must have been extremely frustrating for Norma who perhaps longed to enjoy Bryan at home in full health.

The well-known theatrical phrase from producer to actor, 'Don't ring us, we'll ring you!' is very accurate. An actor turned agent, who had been friendly with Bryan at one time, suddenly rang out of the blue one day and asked if Bryan could come to London. Simon Oakes specialized in casting commercials for film and television, and needed to find the right face to advertize a new potato product. Walking into the office and meeting those responsible, Bryan found a new sense of confidence within himself and the sense that he was to get the job.

He was right. His looks, mannerisms and relaxed but fatherly voice were just what they were looking for. He was to play a modern, professor-type character who was both domestic scientist and community officer. With a long, white coat and a sense of gentle authority, they felt that with the right script he would have no problem in persuading the public to buy their new product. They also wanted him to do some stunts, and he was actually seen in one commercial swinging from a chandelier.

'Albert's crisps' were a novel brand of aerated potato snacks that would make your mouth tingle when eaten. It's an oddity that despite Bryan's inability to learn lines quickly and retain them, nearly 30 years later he can still remember these: 'My name is Albert Watson and I've had this little idea. These are puffed-up crisps, but I don't know what to call them. I hope you'll buy a few, as I've worked very hard to make them.'

He was so convincing that several of the technicians working on the filming actually thought he was the real genius behind the idea. The advert went out on prime-time television and Bryan was very pleased with his new characterization. He even won an award for the television advert, and Morecambe and Wise based one of their funniest television sketches on it.

Suddenly, to the manufacturers' horror, it was discovered that the crisps were not keeping fresh for as long as expected. Complaints of packets going rotten on the shelves were beginning to flood in, and many tons of the product had to be destroyed. New plastic packaging was hastily designed, and the product was placed back in the shops. The manufacturers commissioned a new series of advertisements, and once again Bryan's services were called for. The only problem was that this new packaging was found to be almost impossible to open by its customers, and further advertisements followed featuring Bryan displaying the art of opening these innovative bags.

Sadly, the manufacturers, Vanderburghs, had only just got the product back on its feet when a potato famine hit the market. This meant that their basic ingredient was not now available, or only at a hugely inflated price. They had made such a large outlay on this revolutionary product, including the factory which had cost £1.5 million, that the business could not survive and finally had to be abandoned. It was later sold off to another company, and the aerated crisp product is still a popular part of our everyday diet.

Bryan's income with the advertisements suddenly dried up, just as he was enjoying the fact that his bank account had become more puffed up than the crisps he was advertising. On the strength of 'Albert's', the Mosleys moved to a much bigger house in Shipley, West Yorkshire. It was a fine, five-bedroomed home set at the bottom of a gently sloping hill. They had also managed to get Jacqueline into St Joseph's College in Bradford, a rather exclusive establishment. Simone and Helen went there later, and Bryan was able to pay the fees by giving some extra drama lessons to private pupils from time to time. The headmistress was Sister Wilfred, and her kindness was appreciated by Bryan and Norma, who feel that the girls didn't really know how privileged they were to be there.

Financial panic was about to hit them once more, when Bryan suddenly received a letter from the Inland Revenue demanding a large proportion of the money he had earned from the commercial over the past year. It was a huge tax bill, and the thought of how he could ever pay it sent Bryan spiralling down into a chasm of despondency.

In the past he had never earned enough to pay any tax. He, like many others in the profession, had fallen into the trap of not getting into the habit of putting a percentage of his earnings aside. The money he had was already spent, and with no job, he had no visible means of paying off this new liability. With the help of a local accountant, he eventually came to an arrangement with the Inland Revenue in which the few thousand pounds that he owed was repaid slowly over several years. The burden of this hung over the family like a black cloud for some time. It was a salutary lesson which caused Bryan to be very careful about his savings in the future. He was determined that this situation would not occur again.

Now it seemed that the fame and fortune that Bryan had enjoyed was once again mercilessly snatched away. It was all the more difficult to swallow because it was due to reasons beyond his control. The TV strike and the potato famine were to blame, not a failure on his part to do a good, professional job. So what of the future? Bryan began to despair of ever working on television again. This was made even more painful for him by the letters he received from viewers, asking him if Alf was ever coming back.

Yet within Bryan there is always a glimmer of hope, a candle shining in the darkness, and a determination to try pushing some new doors. His Christian faith was an inspiration to him at times like these, and he would often be seen with head in hands, praying for a way out. 'My faith, like everyone else's, wavers from time to time,' he says. 'In fact it's been at the most difficult and seemingly hopeless times of my life that my faith has helped me through. I have only to recall all the amazing blessings I have received, and the near despair which sometimes seems to grip me like a vice starts to melt away.'

As Bryan started to put his words into action, and felt the threat of despondency evaporate, a new hope began to dawn inside him. He sensed that his future was somehow in firm hands, and that sooner or later something would turn up. After all, it always had before.

9

A Film Career

When asked what he looked for in a film script,
Spencer Tracy replied, 'Days off.'

Since his boyhood Bryan has been passionate about the
cinema, and is forever grateful to his father for introducing him
to the world of films. Jimmy would walk his small son, hand in
hand, to the local Picture Palace, where films would send his
imagination into the sort of orbit which would keep him awake
for several nights in a row.

As a youngster Bryan would carefully save his money so that
he could go to the cinema at least four or five times a week,
often on his own. *King Kong* also had a great impact on Bryan,
frightening him to death. Some films were not intended for
youngsters, and they were not allowed in without an adult
accompanying them. So Bryan would stand outside in the
queue, asking adults if they would take him in with them.
There was always someone to oblige. He could get in for
twopence until he turned 18.

Bryan's love of the cinema always excited him, almost to the
point of obsessiveness. Even when watching a lousy film, the
actors' techniques, the camera angles and the direction would
captivate him. The special effects and, in particular, the fighting
sequences would also enthral him. Action films would frustrate

him because of the continuous cuts made by the film editor, which would prevent him from seeing an actor in sequence.

When the major film director John Schlessinger was casting for his new classic film, *A Kind of Loving*, Bryan jumped at the opportunity to be seen and considered for a part. While willing to consider Bryan for a part in the film, and well aware that he was good enough an actor to make it in films, Schlessinger still had serious reservations about hiring him. Bryan was to learn a new lesson about the flip-side of television fame – that is, the problem of type-casting.

Once an actor has been seen by the public as playing a particular character for long enough, it proves extremely difficult to perceive this person in any other role. This can be very frustrating for adventurous performers, who find themselves suddenly trapped inside the skin of a particular persona, and not given the chance to explore others. There is a saying that suggests, 'If you were in something for longer than six weeks, think again.' While many young actors dream of being type-cast in the sense that it brings fame and financial security, the reality is somewhat different, as its limiting properties soon reveal.

Eventually it becomes a 'Catch-22' situation. The actor is ultimately forced to make a decision whether to continue with the character for a short while and then resign, avoiding type-casting but running the very real risk of not getting further work. The alternative is to stay on for as long as possible, sacrificing the chance of working elsewhere, but still running the risk that the writers might just kill your character off anyway. This situation is at its most obvious in soap operas such as *Coronation Street*. The characters portrayed are presented as real people, and the viewer gets an increasing insight into the lives and interaction of those in the community.

John Schlessinger had instantly recognized Bryan as Alf Roberts and knew that his film audience would do the same. Bryan used all his persuasive skills and was eventually cast in *A Kind of Loving* as a cheerful and kind bus driver. He was later cast by the same director in another classic film, *Billy Liar*, but all his scenes were cut from the finished film.

Some years later Bryan's best friend Derek Ware was choreographing the fight scenes in *Far From the Madding Crowd* for Mr Schlessinger, and he passed on Bryan's regards to the director. Schlessinger immediately asked if Bryan would be interested in coming onto the set to do some fight scenes for the film. Bryan agreed, and travelled to where the film was being made on location.

As in the experience of many actors, it seems, the telephone offering work is either silent or rings all the time. It often happens that after waiting for suitable work to appear, you suddenly get many offers out of the blue. This time it was Albert Finney who rang, asking Bryan to perform in a new film called *Charlie Bubbles*. Explaining that he had just committed himself to a fight scene in *Far From the Madding Crowd*, Bryan had to turn the work down. Some days later, on Bryan's only day off from filming, Mr Finney phoned again, once more trying to persuade Bryan to take part in *Charlie Bubbles*. Agents, casting directors and actors eventually rearranged their filming schedules, and Bryan found himself with two concurrent film contracts in his hands, travelling back and forth between the films' locations in Derbyshire and Dorset.

It was in *Far From the Madding Crowd* that Bryan had greater opportunity to show off his expertise as a stunt fighter. Having been taught by a friend many years earlier, his fights were becoming so realistic that some of those he was working opposite were actually frightened of him. Real terror would

show on their faces when confronted with a highly antago-
nistic Bryan, complete with a three-foot-long blade of steel in
his big hands. Memories of losing his temper during the fight
in the RAF had enabled him to understand how important it
was to enjoy an attack, yet remain in control. He believes that
'Whatever it is that they put you through in an Armed Forces
training course, it's in your blood for ever, but it has to be kept
in check.' The physicality of fighting was particularly appreciated by Bryan, who loved to wrestle more than anything else.

His first fight had been in a production of *Othello* at Perth.
'I had shown an interest in fighting, and they had asked me if I
would be prepared to direct the great fight scene of the play,'
he remembers. 'I agreed, but it went dreadfully wrong, it had
no continuity and looked woefully unrealistic. I was extremely
embarrassed every time we performed it. The actor opposite
me was frightened to death, which didn't help, and I tried to
reassure him that I wasn't really going to hurt him. I reminded
him that there would be no point in me causing him injury, as
we had to do it again the following night! I really didn't know
what I was doing, though, and it was a complete disaster.'

It was with Ian Hendry in a television film called *The High
Game* that Bryan got his first opportunity for a very messy on-
screen brawl. It became one of the longest screen hand-fights,
lasting just over two minutes. Due to the length of the scene
and the energies involved, the bout was performed and
recorded in one 'take'. This was in no small way attributed to
the carefully rehearsed moves that are an essential part of every
fight scene.

In a scene in the BBC TV series *Adam Adamant* the
programme's star, Gerald Harper, gave Bryan a seriously large
black eye. During the actual 'take' the fight had gone wrong
when Gerald had put in an extra and unexpected move. He

had then misjudged a blow to Bryan's head, and had caught him square over his left eye. The scene was finally repeated with plenty of make-up covering Bryan's injury. Returning to the series for yet another fight scene with Mr Harper, the same thing happened again, causing Bryan to say, 'Gerry, if you hurt me once more, I shall kick you so bloody hard you'll wonder what happened to you!'

Bryan recalls, 'He did the same thing again, so I kicked him hard in the shins, but he never said anything about it. I'm very fond of Gerry, but I had no respect for his fighting ability. On another occasion he was determined to jump dangerously onto a table. He rehearsed it with his glasses on, took them off for the take, jumped, missed his footing and went down as the whole table collapsed beneath him.'

Bryan, who was credited in these films with tongue-in-cheek stunt names such as Dexter Burk, Alf Hart or Buddy Windrush, has very little respect for most fight scenes these days. 'The public is not fooled so much because, due to the pressure of budgets, not enough time, thought and energy is put into fights. Actors think they can just turn up, do a quick rehearsal and make it look real. The basic training is also often missing. Fencing was an essential part of my training at drama school. In my early days it was Errol Flynn and Basil Rathbone who did the most amazing sword fights, making the audiences flinch at their antics. One of my biggest regrets is not doing more fencing on screen, although I have taught a lot of other actors to fence. Lots of actors are frightened of fencing, and it's hard to convince them that you are not going to kill them. Once they have mastered the art, they have the basic skill and understanding to present any fight convincingly.

'The real secret of making a fight look real is to put little accidents and slips in that seem unplanned. In directing one television fight, for example, I asked one of the actors if he could possibly slip up on a stone step and end up in a very bad position as his assailant followed. He did it well, and the film crew gasped in shock.' One of Bryan's best memories is the time when he taught some schoolchildren to fight as part of a school project they were doing. It became so successful that it still operates as a semi-professional theatre school of fencing for children to this day.

Derek Ware also remembers what a good swordsman Bryan was. 'Despite his weight, he was extremely agile on his feet, and could move like a dancer. I always told the drama students I taught that they should not be in competition with their opponent, but should think of themselves as Fred Astaire and Ginger Rogers. It's a carefully choreographed routine. Bryan was just like that. Not that he didn't make mistakes, though. Some of our biggest rows were when Bryan would think up a great new move like a punch or a back-slap, and it would go wrong, and I'd get a fist round the back of my head. He was extremely inventive, always thinking up new ideas for fights.

'Somehow Bryan is a good all-rounder. He is a great actor, but loves a bit of action too. He loved the dangerous side to his work. Having worked as a stunt man most of my life, I can see the dangers as well as the financial benefits. For example, if I was employed to do a fall off a building I would be paid £1 per foot that I fell. The cardboard boxes that stunt men would fall onto would cost 7s. 6d., and this was quite a lot of money in those days. As we had to buy them ourselves, the temptation was to try to save money, but if you went too short on boxes, you could get injured. Nowadays stunt men can earn up to £1 million for just one film, and can retire on the proceeds.'

The art of filming, however, is not nearly as glamorous as it seems. A typical example was when Bryan was offered a part in the classic Robert Louis Stevenson story *Treasure Island*. 'I was looking forward to it, as it was to be filmed in the Canary Islands. Thoughts of relaxing in the sun while waiting for the shoot filled my mind. But then the venue was changed to the Channel Islands and then to Devon, where it poured with rain the whole time. Our costumes seemed to be continuously damp, and an old actor called Reg Lye used to build huge fires on the beach each day to try and dry them off.

'We also ate huge amounts of the biggest wild blackberries I've ever seen, and the ship they were filming on, *The Hispaniola*, nearly sank. Peter Vaughan was Long John Silver. It was a very uncomfortable time, though in the end the film looked great. It was one of the last films made in black and white.'

During the making of *Far From the Madding Crowd* Mr Schlessinger had asked Bryan to ad lib an additional scene in his film. After the scene was shot, the great director put his arm around Bryan, saying, 'We might not be able to keep your scene in the film, but I'll make sure they see it in Hollywood.'

True to his word, Bryan got full billing on the film titles, and when Hollywood moguls were casting *Get Carter* in 1971, they were shown this piece of additional footage to see what Bryan was like. This led him to be offered the role in this enduring but violent adult thriller, which is still shown several times a year on television.

'They had Telly Savalas in mind for the part originally, but they obviously thought I was a bit harder looking! I played the part of the gangster Brumby. On the day when they fitted me up with my suit in London, the costume fitter said he had just measured my stunt double for his clothes too, and we were remarkably alike.'

The film was to have a quite distinguished cast list which included Michael Caine, Ian Hendry, Britt Ekland, George

Sewell, John Osborne and Bernard Hepton. Film critic John Patterson describes the film as one of the all-time classics. 'Leslie Halliwell's *Film and Video Viewer Guide* dismisses *Get Carter* as a "brutal British crime melodrama. Sex and thuggery unlimited, narrative disjointed, rewards few." I'd agree with every syllable of that, except "few". The rewards are legion. Britt Ekland as Audrey, for instance. She's only in one scene. When they cut the movie for television, she only appears in the credits!

'The gangster factions in *Get Carter*, led by Cyril Kinnear [played by John Osborne] and Cliff Brumby [played by Bryan] are only shades away from these real-life figures. Indeed, Carter throws Brumby to his death from the fifth floor of one of his own half-built granite-and-glass monstrosities. Brumby's death is only one of many killings in the film.

'Roy Budd's score, an echo-laden collage of stinging, chimelike pianos and electric guitars, keeps the audience on tenterhooks throughout, while Wolfgang Suschitsky's photography is vividly sleazy, exactly capturing the gloom of the industrial North-East, with its grey skies and unceasing rain. The sun doesn't shine once in *Get Carter*. The last time I saw *Get Carter* was also the first time I'd seen it on the big screen, at the infamous Nuart Theater in Santa Monica. The print was excellent, and seeing it full-size, I realized how skilfully it's framed and edited. A few rows in front of me sat Quentin Tarantino, who didn't bother to stay for the other half of the double bill, Robert Altman's *The Long Goodbye*. His presence made sense when I read Pauline Kael's original review of *Carter*: "So calculatedly cool and soulless and nastily erotic that it seems to belong to a new era of virtuoso viciousness." Without this and other movies in the same vein, *Reservoir Dogs* and *Pulp Fiction* might never have found their inspiration.'

So what was a nice guy like Bryan Mosley doing in a violently brutal film like this? It was initially very confusing when two *Get Carter* film scripts arrived through Bryan's letterbox. They were for two different parts, and Bryan had been offered the small cameo role of 'Arthur'. The inevitable phone call came, and a voice from the studio told him to throw the 'Arthur' part away, as he was now being offered the lead part of Brumby. This brought tears to Bryan's eyes. He thought it was a joke at first, then grasped the role with both hands and knew that he would give the role everything he had got.

'It was a fantastic opportunity to be part of such a well-written film, but I was very aware of the violence, and for a moment I wondered if I should allow myself to be part of it.' In fact he decided to take good advice from someone he knew would be good at looking at this problem from the right angle. 'I went straight to my local priest and showed him the script. He took a while to read it, and I waited anxiously for his verdict. I was thrilled to be part of the film, but if it compromised my faith in any way, I knew I would be willing to drop it. A few days later the priest returned with his conclusion. I was pretty astounded when he said he thought that it was a very good morality play! The tone of the piece, although violent, did not condone such actions – indeed, even condemned them. I was relieved and at peace with the decision to go ahead.'

It was filmed in Newcastle, and Bryan found himself working alongside some of the biggest names in Hollywood, like Michael Caine, who was already a three-time Oscar nominee. 'Unfortunately one of my favourite scenes, in which I have a serious punch-up with Michael Caine, was cut from the final version. This was because they decided that Caine should be the killer who never gets hurt until the end, when he gets a bullet between the eyes.'

The film critics loved it. '*Excellent!* Violent, sexy, exciting, honest!' is how the *Los Angeles Herald-Examiner* reviewed the picture. 'The pace is relentless,' said the *L.A. Times*, 'and picks up momentum like a freight train barrelling downgrade!' 'An instant classic,' agreed the *New York Times*, 'and quite ferociously erotic!' 'Brutal and gamy plot turns, excellent direction, a fast-moving screenplay,' said *Variety*.

That the film became such a classic is evident in the fact that 25 years later the film is being advertised using the latest marketing techniques on the Internet. The 'Mr Showbiz' guide says:

Caine rips into 'his best role in years' in this vigorous crime thriller marked by London mob strong-arm Jack Carter. [Caine] is drawn north to Newcastle by his brother's death – which he doesn't believe is accidental. All too familiar with the ways of the mob, Carter single-mindedly – and single-handedly – tears into the local crime syndicate with terrifying precision and cold enjoyment, hunting the identity of the killer and then the killer himself. But what Carter doesn't know is that the corruption within the mob is widespread, high-ranked, and may hit closer to home than he thinks. For heart-thumping, knuckle-whitening, can't-take-your-eyes-off-the-screen entertainment, *Get Carter*!'

Even on such timeless films as these Bryan remains the perfectionist, always judging his performance and often wishing he could have done things better. Nevertheless, *Get Carter* firmly established him as an essential part of MGM history, as shown in their book *The MGM Story*, and he is forever grateful to Director Roy Hodges, who also wrote the script.

Showbusiness is cruel, however, and no matter how good your performance, it is the overall success of a production which raises or lowers your personal chances of future work. For Bryan the main result of the film's acceptance was that doors offering a new and exciting career in films began to open, and the pressure on Bryan to pursue a Hollywood film career now sprang into action, with invitations coming from every direction. He was faced with making one of the most difficult decisions of his life. To go to America and see if all these promises of work were true, or to carve a career in England.

The decision was, in some ways, already made. Bryan had always found it difficult to feel relaxed away from home. Trying to keep work and home life very separate in his mind, he would anticipate with some eagerness the end of a week's filming so that he could get back home to the family. 'My heart was always with Norma, and I felt very selfish being away from her. I knew I had to choose between her and the family, or a new career abroad. I couldn't have both. I chose to stay, and I've never regretted it.'

It was while Bryan was considering a Hollywood film career that he felt he once again needed higher help in making the difficult decision to turn down something that he had always dreamed of. Entering a small local church, he sat alone on the wooden pew and prayed for guidance. Once more, he desperately wanted God to show him a way forward.

There were no flashes of lighting, nor angelic voices, but later that day the phone rang. 'A voice at the other end told me that they wanted Alf Roberts back.' He had his answer.

10

Life on the *Street*

'There was life before *Coronation Street*,
but it didn't amount to much.'
Russell Harty

When Bryan arrived back at Granada Television in 1968, after a break of nearly seven years, he found that many things had changed. The television strike which had forced his departure earlier was well forgotten, and the atmosphere on the *Street* was different too. No longer was there a sense of bewilderment and muddling through under any circumstances. The *Street* had become a well-oiled piece of machinery, esteemed by all involved. It had become Granada's flagship and was given the status and protection that it deserved. It had certainly come a long way since its inception.

'Doomed from the outset' was how the *Daily Mail*'s top television critic initially saw the new soap series, because of its 'grim scene of a row of terraced houses and smoking chimneys'.

By the time Bryan arrived back, it was regularly topping the audience ratings, and over the next 20 years was to claim more than 100 million viewers world-wide across six continents; 15 million of these were in the UK alone. *Coronation Street* had become the most popular soap opera in Britain, and was destined to become the world's longest-running television drama serial. Somehow Bryan sensed he was part of a success story that knew no bounds.

Graham Alsop, one of the *Street*'s most ardent fans, says that, like other UK soaps, its attraction lies in the mundane. 'Set in the fictional Weatherfield, part of the Manchester conurbation in north-west England, it portrays ordinary working-class people in ordinary, believable situations, and is a world away from US soaps such as *Dallas* and *Dynasty*. However, what makes the *Street* stand out from other UK soaps is the quality of writing, and the fact that plots are written from the characters' viewpoint, rather than the issue-led storylines of other soaps.'

Coronation Street was the brainchild of the writer Tony Warren. Although he was brought up in middle-class surroundings in Swinton, Manchester, Warren drew inspiration from his grandmother's surroundings in inner-city Manchester. In 1956, Warren, then only 19, wrote *Where No Birds Sing*, a script about a northern back street, and a year later he developed a comedy version called *Our Street* which he submitted to the BBC in Leeds and which, famously, is still awaiting a reply. In 1958 he joined Granada Television, writing episodes for *Shadow Squad*, *People and Places* and *Biggles*.

Granada Television (named after the Spanish city) had been created by the brothers Sydney and Cecil Bernstein in 1955, and was granted a licence to transmit television in the North of England. Part of the remit was to reflect the life of the region, but they were hardly fulfilling this. After he had pressurized the producer, Harry Elton, to let him write about something he knew and understood, Warren was given 24 hours to 'come up with an idea to take Britain by storm'. Drawing on his child-hood experiences and those first two scripts, he produced overnight what was to become the first episode of *Coronation Street*. Its potential was immediately obvious, and Warren's memo to the Granada board, explaining *Florizel Street* (*Coronation Street*'s working title), ensured its production:

> A fascinating freemasonry, a volume of unwritten rules. These are the driving forces behind life in a working-class street in the North of England. The purpose of *Florizel Street* is to examine a community of this nature, and to entertain.

Coronation Street went into production initially with 12 episodes, and a possible extra final episode, where the street was literally to be bulldozed if the programme wasn't successful. The first episode was transmitted at 7 p.m. on Friday 9 December 1960 and was an immediate success. Before the end of 1960, more episodes were commissioned, and by May 1961 it was fully networked throughout the UK, topping the TV ratings – where it has remained ever since.

The characters of the *Street* have always been the central theme for any scriptwriter, and the gap left by Bryan's earlier departure must have been noticed, as it was decided that the character of Alf should be reinstated as an essential part of life on the *Street*. It was 1968, and Bryan resumed his place in the country's top soap while surrounded by the drama of the day. It was a year of shock and sadness, marked by the assassination of both Dr Martin Luther King and Senator Robert Kennedy. The Beatles had just made their film *Yellow Submarine* and opened their first 'Apple' boutique. The American millionaire oil tycoon Robert McCullough bought London Bridge for £1 million, only to discover when he got it back home that it wasn't the one he had expected. Significantly, it was also the year when the first successful heart transplant was performed in London.

British television was now in full swing. Sooty had moved from the BBC to Thames, and 'soaps' – domestic light drama series – were in abundance. Some were even being sponsored by soap manufacturers. *Coronation Street* now had a firm place in the hearts of millions, and Bryan's return coincided with the first week when the show would be transmitted in colour. Despite the profound sense of purpose and direction to be found at Granada, he quickly discovered that some of the old problems still hadn't been resolved. It would still be trans- mitted live. With the greater ease in which film was devel- oping, alongside the onset of commercial videotape, many other TV serials were now being recorded. Fewer television dramas continued to put their cast through the stress of a live performance. As far as the *Coronation Street* management were concerned, however, there was the fear that to stop the programme going out live would rob it of a certain edge of tension in the drama.

Many of the cast were becoming increasingly exhausted by this tension, and several of the most established characters even threatened to leave the show if it continued in this way. Violet Carson, who played Ena Sharples, confessed privately to Bryan one day that she could 'not carry on like this much longer'. Some directors were liked by the cast, and others were disliked because they displayed no real respect for the actors. Bryan admits that they were treated like puppets sometimes. Some of the early producers of the programme were particularly hard to work with. The cast understood that they were under some pressure to get the show out, but this would often cause the director to become quite distant on a personal basis and a bit of a slave-driver. The cast complained that some of the directors seemed to see all the performers as characters and not as real people.

Bryan says, 'We were all working very, very hard, and were expected to be on call 24 hours a day, seven days a week. People who think that working as an actor on a TV soap like this is easy, need to think again! We had a very tight schedule which used to be a killer, and you would never know what you were doing from week to week. I could never plan more than a few days ahead. This meant I had practically no family or social life whatsoever. The cast would become exhausted very quickly, and some would become ill and would still be expected to come in. How we kept the pace up I shall never know, as we could hardly find time for real life. Constantly on call and asked to open fêtes and attend other events, even when we weren't supposed to be working, seemed to take all our time. We were expected to stay on call in the studio all day and every day. Some days I would sit in the lounge there and never be called in to record anything at all. Pat Phoenix and Violet Carson and others put up with sharing tiny dressing-rooms, which was both irksome and frustrating. We seemed to be waiting for a train to arrive, until one day we realized that we were already on it and going nowhere. Sooner or later some people rebelled. The producers began to listen, and gradually things started to improve.'

Bryan's capacity to be bold enabled him to have no fear in terms of confronting the management with situations that he felt were unfair and unjust. He considered his initial offer of a six-month contract with a three-year 'get out' on the *Street* as unfair on the part of the management. It had meant that they could call on Bryan's services for up to three years without having to change his fee, and with the option of sacking him after six months if they didn't like him. This led Bryan to re-negotiate his own contract. He faced the management in their office and declared that he wasn't going to have more than a one-year contract, and he wanted to negotiate his own fee. They didn't believe him at first, and Bryan nearly lost the job by refusing to change his position. Once they realized that he was serious, Bryan became even bolder in asking for a retainer.

Often a television contract will forbid an actor to work anywhere else during the run of his contract, which also means that he doesn't earn anything if he is not used by the television company. Bryan considers this a very unfair agreement because the restriction of not being able to work anywhere else could have serious financial implications over which you had no power. You also faced the possibility of sitting at home for several weeks without payment if the script-writers decided not to use your character for a while.

Bryan remembers that 'I took a great risk by digging my heels in on this subject and refused to change my position. In the end they agreed to my demands, everybody else on the *Street* got the same deal, and I am pleased to be responsible for something that has benefited many television actors since.'

Bryan also breathed a sigh of relief mixed with great optimism. He had finally achieved a certain measure of the sort of security that he had never enjoyed in his profession before – the type of security that most other people in their nine-to-five jobs often take for granted. Now he could look forward to a monthly pay packet that he knew would be there for several months ahead.

In fact Bryan was to draw an uninterrupted wage from Granada for the next 20 years, and settled down to life as a soap star. In Bryan's usual way, he was not one to take the weekly wage for granted, and although most of the problems had been ironed out, there was always the worry that a character could suddenly disappear.

The possibility of being written out by the whim of a script-writer looking for extra drama was always out of Bryan's hands, of course, but the fear always lurked around the corner. Every week Bryan would wonder if it would be his last, particularly at a time when the script was not very complimentary to him, and it seemed that all his lines were there just to lead into other people's stories. At first he had been reluctant to come back, and certainly wouldn't have done if he had known that he would be there for so long. 'It was a very deceptive way for an actor to work, as you would become all nice and comfortable with a steady job, and then the rug would suddenly be pulled out from under you whenever the script-writer decided to change your character. It would bring out all the deep insecurities within you.'

It is rumoured that Margot Bryant, who played Minnie Caldwell, became obsessed with a fear of being written out of the series. When the weekly script arrived at her home she was in the habit of ripping it open and glancing through the last few pages, 'just to see if they've killed me off yet!' This she did regularly for more than 14 years. Ironically, in 1969 her character was nearly killed in a coach crash, and the following year Minnie was held at gunpoint by her lodger, Joe Donnelli. She was eventually written out in 1976 when her character left after accepting a job as a housekeeper to an old friend in Whaley Bridge, a small village south-east of Manchester.

The *Street*, recorded seven days a week at Manchester's Granada TV complex, was also in the years to come more frequently filmed out on location anywhere within driving distance. As the show developed and became more and more popular, much was expected from the limited production facilities, and the old studios could simply not cope with all the new demands. The *Street* sets would have to be dismantled regularly to allow other productions studio space, and it was eventually decided that the series deserved its own permanent studio complex.

The purpose-built studios resembled a smart, red-brick-fronted office block, ironically built on original Mancunian cobblestones. Set in their own grounds, the studios enjoy an outside set of the Street itself, shared with the Granada studios tour, a multi-million-pound television theme park which sprang up in the early nineties and provides Granada with a handsome amount of extra revenue. When the outside Street set is not being used for the series, visitors from the theme park can walk down Britain's most famous street for themselves, and imagine they are part of the Weatherfield community. Her Majesty the Queen, herself an ardent watcher of the programme, once visited the set and met the cast, including Bryan, who talked to her for some time. 'I noticed that she was always moving,' he says. 'She would chat, then move away, only to return a few moments later. I wondered if she did this for security reasons. We chatted about all sorts of things, including life on the *Street* and my own family, but somehow we ended our conversation with a discussion about the usefulness of Damart underwear!' Bryan was later to meet the Queen again when he collected his OBE for 'Services to the Community'.

The close vicinity of the theme park to the Granada studio complex meant that the cast of *Coronation Street* became increasingly under scrutiny from the public whenever they stepped out from the security and privacy of the studio block itself. Fans waiting at the big iron gates hoped to catch a glimpse of their favourite TV stars, despite a large notice politely asking members of the public to give consideration to the performers and let them have free access. The reaction of the crowds was always different depending on who they could see. A huge scream reminiscent of the teenybopper age would resound for the latest young heart-throb actor as he crossed the yard, whilst a hundred hands would wave reverently at Bryan when he made an appearance. It all goes to show how much the series crossed the age and gender barriers of its viewers.

Although the fans were mostly welcomed, it caused problems too. This was particularly true at meal breaks, which would involve the actors and actresses having to battle their way out of the main gates past the fans to the TV club building opposite, in order to get lunch. The new building had not been provided with its own catering facilities, and many considered this to be something that had been badly overlooked. The whole scenario of taking a break would be difficult for the cast, who just wanted to relax in their few minutes of rest from filming. The problem of free access was eventually made easier with the introduction of portable catering facilities parked on the cobblestones directly outside the studio itself. However, the Portakabin kitchen which served the food and the full-length coach complete with tables and seats were somehow at odds with the luxury of the studios themselves.

Inside the complex a comfortable 'Green Room' provided coffee, tea and hot chocolate on tap – the strongest beverages available! Crates and kegs of beer stood in the corner of the small kitchen area for the use of 'The Rovers Return' only. Bryan enjoys a drink, but is not that fond of beer. He was glad that the mixture they used on the *Street* wasn't beer any more, as it had been in the early days. He used to get very amused as the cast got slowly tipsy as filming progressed. Then they changed it to dandelion and burdock, but the cast all suffered from stomach bugs once when they didn't clean the pipes properly. Now it was shandy, which seemed to suit everybody.

The constant stream of hot drinks and biscuits in the Green Room helped to stem the boredom while waiting around for each scene to be recorded. Bryan felt it was reminiscent of a doctor's waiting room, with some nervous actors pacing the floor, muttering through their lines at the last minute to make sure they could remember them. When the amber flashing light went on, it was the signal that recording had started, and only those involved with that particular scene should go through the double steel doors into the studio area itself. Once the flashing stopped, indicating that recording had paused and the director was happy with it, the floor manager would call out the names of the actors required for the next scene.

With recording taking place approximately four weeks ahead of screening, Bryan would shuffle his way into the studio each day, and sit at the bar of the Rovers wearing the usual worried expression that Alf was famed for. One script suggested a scene in which the landlord, Alec Gilroy (played by actor Roy Barraclough), tried to introduce a portable television into the bar for the use of the regulars. The residents, however, were not at all happy about this – particularly Alf, who did not want his local to be spoiled by the intrusion of a noisy television. The exact placing of the television by the actor was a problem for the camera crew trying to line up the shot, and alongside a host of other minor problems, it caused Bryan's four lines to take over an hour to record successfully.

Technical problems are the chink in the armour of Bryan, a man who under most other circumstances is very patient. Misplaced lighting, a sudden noise or a missing prop were certain to get Bryan mumbling to himself crossly. Contented with huffing and puffing and rolling his eyes when the same scene had to be repeated several times over, he was unlikely to storm off set, like many others were known to have done. After several years of taking silent deep breaths when the technical problems arose, he once burst out, 'Oh, come on, luvvies – this is theatre, you know!' It became a regular cliché used by Bryan and his screen wife played by Sue Nicholls.

The story-line itself was always kept as a closely guarded secret, with Bryan and other members of the cast signing a secrecy clause preventing them from revealing the contents of their scripts to anyone outside the studio. Once the recorded scene was played back to the satisfaction of the director, Bryan was free to leave the studio and make his way back to his private dressing-room. Past the walls covered with framed pictures of the *Street* over the years, his room is sandwiched between Barbara Knox (who plays Rita Sullivan) and Helen Worth (who plays Gail Platt), who describes Bryan as 'every child's perfect grandfather. Warm, cuddly and, most of all, he's fun.'

The dressing-room was Bryan's oasis of tranquillity and isolation, and he loved it, feeling at home in his own space. No one else used his dressing-room. It was totally his, and he probably spent more of his time there than anywhere else. The way his room was kept says much about his character.

With two official-looking in-trays overflowing with letters, and several piles more on the counter, it gave the impression that he would benefit from a secretary. Bryan would admit that 'It's pretty much a mess, muddled and untidy, but that's the way I feel sometimes. Always something more to do. Never being able to get at the bottom of something.'

The most frustrating thing about being a public figure is suffering a loss of identity. Bryan gets annoyed when people expect him to be somebody he is not. The general public see him as Alf most of the time, and Bryan describes their reactions as 'silly' and is constantly amazed by the endless amount of fan mail he receives, being particularly irritated by those who address him as 'Alf'. 'I just can't understand how people could be so stupid as to think that *Coronation Street* is real. I mean, I would even get people writing to me to ask if they could purchase certain items of food they had seen in Alf's shop. There was a shortage of salt once, and I had several people ask if I could send them some of mine. In the early days we were not allowed to use real brand names in the shop, as it would be seen as unfair advertising. The product's logo either had to be covered up in some way, or we had to invent our own. We invented the name "Key", and soon afterwards some enterprising manufacturer decided to use this name for a chain of corner shops.'

Appeals to attend charity functions came at the rate of 30 a week, but petitions for items of clothing were also a regular addition to his mailbag. One lady even asked him for a pair of Alf's underpants once, but the usual request is for a tie. Often auctioning these items to raise money for charity, the saddest thing for Bryan is that in all the years of helping people with their requests, only one person wrote back to thank him. It reminds him of the biblical story where Jesus heals 12 men and only one returns to show his gratitude. 'I suppose many people see us on the box every week, and presume that we are public property. I can understand that, but I sometimes wish that viewers had a little more respect.' This treatment also heightens the frustration he feels when he is not being recognized or remembered as a good actor in anything besides the *Street*. His dressing-room reflected this disappointment in his choice of personal decoration.

The wall above his desk had the obligatory mirror framed with lights, and the remainder was covered with all types of cards, photos, bits of paper bearing important telephone numbers, and a decorative cross. The Queen and several pictures of his heroes Laurel and Hardy also adorned the wall. 'I love Laurel and Hardy because they make me laugh so much with their incredibly clever comic timing. Stan and Ollie still have the ability to make me cry with laughter. Since I was very small, I always loved their amazing antics, and would dearly love to have been born as Ollie. Whenever I felt low and in need of being cheered up, I would watch one of their films – even one I may have seen a thousand times before – and I'm instantly transported from gloom to pure joy. After Hardy's death in 1957 I would write to Stanley on a regular basis. Inconsolable after his partner's passing, he refused to resume performing, although he continued writing until his own death in 1965. We became quite good pen-pals, and when my sixth child was born, he wrote back and said, 'Well done – the birth of a nation!'

Bryan's regrets over never having had the opportunity to do more comedy were also reflected in a treasured photo which stood out above the rest. Sir Laurence Olivier was symbolic of the very finest in the art of acting as far as Bryan was concerned. A hint of jealousy tinged with a rueful lament over lost opportunities still fill Bryan's mind on occasions. He bemoans the fact that in some ways, his time on the *Street* has robbed him of the chance to go on to prove his abilities with greater theatrical performances, and maybe Hollywood too. Sending Sir Laurence a framed playing card with Olivier's picture as Henry V one day, Bryan was thrilled when he received a warm reply. Olivier had written, 'It is fascinating to think of being shuffled and dealt!'

Soon afterwards Olivier requested Bryan to appear in his new television production of *Hindlewakes*. Bryan was to jump at the chance too soon, for, being exclusively contracted to Granada, he was duly forced to decline the offer. Naturally, Bryan was extremely distressed at this decision, but producer Bill Podmore persuaded Bryan that it would not be in anyone's best interests for Alf to be seen as anything else but 'himself'.

Some consolation came when Olivier asked Bryan to work on the programme as a dialect coach. Bryan was able to experience the pleasure of working alongside his hero by squeezing in time during short breaks from the *Street*, and he had great fun. He was asked to address the great actor as 'Sir Laurence'. Apparently he loathed being called 'My Lord'.

Other allegorical emblems on the walls of the dressing-room revealed the character of the real man behind the grocer's coat. The bright-red badge with the words 'Smile! It makes people wonder what you've been up to!' was fastened to the wall alongside Proverbs 3:5, 'Trust in the Lord with all your heart. Never rely on what you think you know', a constant reminder to Bryan of the faith he followed and held dear, even at work.

There was no window in his dressing-room, but the lack of view was supplemented by a whole collection of personal pictures, photos and postcards of holidays. His favourite, a picture of the family posing together, complemented an older photograph of their wedding day, showing the huge white rose adorning Bryan's buttonhole, and Norma's magnificent dress. A whole box full of photographs with Bryan smiling as Alf would sit permanently on the floor, ready to be signed and sent out. He would get annoyed and frustrated at having to sign so many autographs, but it never showed. Bryan started to collect other examples of the way in which his face was used to make money. With the number of viewers and fans ever increasing, merchandise was becoming a big money-spinner for Granada, and it wasn't long before Alf could be seen on anything from T-shirts to tea-cups and drip-mats to jigsaws. Bryan's face adorning the famous Blackpool illuminations was added some years later to advertise a *Coronation Street* exhibition on the promenade. It was here that Alf's face was immortalized in wax as a main feature of the display.

A colourful photograph of Alf in full Mayoral chain and costume smiled back alongside gifts sent in by fans, including a small bust of Sir Winston Churchill peering towards the open-plan wardrobe bulging with several of Alf's jackets, shirts and trousers. Bryan would sometimes have difficulty remembering which clothes he wore for the last scene he recorded, and would refer to the floor manager for help. The pile of shoes in the corner would make it difficult to open the tiny fridge containing several cans of cola, some sparkling water, and a bottle of Chardonnay, which Bryan always kept handy in case of unexpected visitors, or in time of personal need.

A small but gleaming white sink in the corner was where Bryan would dampen down his hair and have his daily wet shave in preparation for Alf's appearances. A fake Oscar with the words 'Best Winger and adequate acting' stood sparkling nearby. 'I awarded myself the trophy to cheer me up one day,' he admits.

By the mid 1970s Bryan had developed the character of Alf as a little 'tongue in cheek' and would often use the character to 'send up' people who are like him. 'I tried to stop him being a caricature, which would be an easy trap to fall into when playing him. Alf was well-intentioned and always trying to do people a good turn, but so often got it totally wrong.' Over the years, Bryan was to stop Alf from doing certain things which he did not personally agree with. At one point the writers wanted Alf to smoke cigarettes, and Bryan resolutely refused, appalled at the thought that it might encourage young people watching to pick up the habit and that he would be held responsible for this. After playing the character for so long, however, it became difficult for Bryan to analyse Alf's motivation too deeply when pushed by the press. 'I just do him,' he would smile.

Bryan saw the apparent lack of adequate air-conditioning in his room as an opportunity to invest in his own fan one hot summer. It sat on a small wicker-work coffee table emitting a gentle breeze which helped him to feel less claustrophobic about the smallness of the space around him, and brought a smile to his face. An Anglepoise lamp would hover over a comfy armchair where Bryan would sit reading, while awaiting his next call to the studio. The books in his room were almost exclusively showbusiness biographies. Bing Crosby sat beside Morecambe and Wise, whose book *Two of a Kind* ironically announces that their TV series in 1963 was 'second in the ratings only to *Coronation Street*'.

The only other significant book is a copy of a Gideon Bible, placed there when the organization Christians in Entertainment held monthly Bible studies in Bryan's dressing-room. In fact CIE opened the doors for Gideons International to place their Bibles in every dressing-room on the *Street* when the new block was opened in 1992. These regular meetings in Bryan's room were a real strength to him, and to the others who joined in, and served as a reminder to him that 'God was interested in every part of my life. Not just when I went to church.'

Huddled together in the tiny room during scene breaks, they would discuss a Bible verse relevant to the profession and pray for the cast, writers and producers of the series. Bryan firmly believed that prayer changes things, and when other members of the cast asked him what they should do in the difficult circumstances they found themselves in, he would sometimes give advice, but always offered to pray for them. He was never a 'Bible-basher', however, and always waited for others to bring up the subject of his faith if they wanted to discuss it with him. Bryan would find that people's perception of God was often wrong, particularly when they saw him as a boring old spoilsport, and Bryan would gleefully remind them that Jesus' first miracle was to change water into wine at a party! Bryan's faith was always respected by other members of the cast and by his peers in the profession. The final guest on his *This is Your Life*, actress Kathy Staff (alias Nora Batty), summed it all up when she said, 'I would like to say, as a fellow Christian, how lovely it is to work with someone so committed to their faith as Bryan. He's such a lovely, honest, genuine man, and to work with him is a pure joy.'

Also respected was his distaste for foul language. Even mild expletives were frowned upon by Bryan. By contrast, he was something of an expert when it came to telling an outrageous story or two!

Bryan shared a great sense of comradeship with his colleagues at Granada, but occasionally found this friendship broken through circumstances that he described as being 'let down'. During the height of the fame of the character Len Fairclough, Peter Adamson, the actor who played him, was beset with a serious problem. Bryan explains that 'Peter would come into the studio first thing in the morning with the smell of drink on his breath. Sometimes he would not be able to stand up properly and say his lines. They asked me to cover for him, but I just felt that was not right, and it wasn't my job.'

Nevertheless, Bryan felt enormous compassion for Peter Adamson, and even telephoned his wife, asking her to encourage Peter to seek help from an alcohol clinic. 'He eventually started to attend Alcoholics Anonymous, and I even went with him at first to try and support him. The look of total shock and surprise on the other victims' faces when they saw us both was very memorable.'

Bryan stood by Peter throughout this trauma, and when Peter faced charges of indecently assaulting young girls in swimming pools, he continued to be by his side, encouraging and befriending him. 'The police evidence against him was hopeless but the news of Peter's charges and his alcoholic problem were in all the daily newspapers over a very long period. The poor man was in a dreadful state while having the problems of his private life spread across the tabloids, and it made me very angry when I saw how much the intrusion of the press can help to destroy a person.'

Torn between staying loyal to a friend and being unwilling to lie, Bryan was forced to make several hard decisions. 'I had a telephone call from his solicitor asking me if I would give a character reference as evidence on Peter's behalf. I told him I couldn't, having seen him offer my own children cigarettes, and he knew how much I hated the smoking habit.'

The charges against Peter Adamson were eventually quashed, but it was only when he sold his story to the newspapers that Bryan felt he could no longer befriend him. 'A man from the press took Peter out and wined and dined him. I imagine he got Peter drunk and encouraged him to tell his story and earn a lot of money for both of them. I was deeply upset that Peter could betray himself in this way, and let everybody in *Coronation Street* down by his behaviour. I'm afraid I lost respect for him. I still have a lot of warm feelings towards him, but it still hurts when I think about what happened and the devastating effect that the stress of it all had on his family. We have written to each other since, though, and I never regret helping him in his time of need, though there are many deep wounds in our relationship.

'The final straw was when the local paper rang me up to ask my opinion on the positive outcome of the case. I simply said that I was pleased for his wife. The headline the next morning, however, read, "Bryan Mosley says, 'I knew my friend was innocent!'" They had totally misquoted and distorted everything I had said. I rang them up and told them that they had printed a pack of lies, and asked if they would please retract what they had printed, but they refused. There was nothing I could do about it, and it has taken a very long time to come to terms with this injustice.'

These experiences caused Bryan to be extremely cautious when talking to the press, and he frowned at other *Street* stars who sold their stories to newspapers. Lynne Perrie, who played Ivy Tilsley, also sold her private story. 'I have no respect for such activities, believing it brings down the integrity of an actor and his character. You must love and respect the person you are playing, and not abuse it,' says Bryan.

More often than not, celebrities have no real control over what the newspapers print anyway. The old showbiz adage which says, 'Today I'm in the newspaper, but tomorrow it will be used for fish and chips', does not always help to heal the deep hurt when you are talked about publicly in this way. One *Street* resident apparently bought a copy of one of the tabloids because 'I wanted to see who I was reported as kissing yesterday!'

Bryan is relieved that his characterization of Alf did not bring the attention of the press to his door that often. In latter days, Bryan would find that when he did any interview with the papers, a press representative from Granada would sit in with him. Unless the reporter was personally known, the cast never really felt they could trust the press. He still made it a rule that he would not reveal too much personal information about himself or the other people with whom he worked and relaxed. He accepted that it was inevitable that some people would see him as public property, but he was still fiercely protective of his right to privacy.

This was often extremely difficult to achieve, and Bryan found that he could not go shopping or even go abroad without being noticed and constantly approached by the public. 'They feel they know me personally because I enter their living-room three times a week,' says Bryan. 'When I went to Disneyland it was crazy. It seemed that people were more interested in me than Mickey Mouse! I think most people leave you alone, but I am always aware of being constantly watched, on public display, which means it's sometimes hard to relax outside my own home. I'm not angry about this – I understand that Alf is quite a popular character, and I accept this as part of the job.'

Some of the more unpopular *Street* characters sometimes experience personal threats by the general public. 'The character of Len Fairclough, who was a bit of a bully on the show, was always getting shouted at in public. I would act as his bouncer sometimes if we went out together.'

With his day at the studio over, and Alf's clothes safely hung up, Bryan would put his wedding ring back on, removing it from his pocket handkerchief, to which it had been secured every day since 1968. Alf never wore a ring, so it was very important to remember to take his off when filming, and more importantly for Bryan, to remember to put it back on afterwards.

Bryan would lock his room, say goodbye to anybody left in the studio and emerge into the sunlight. The fans would still be gathered at the main gate, and several of the show's younger stars would walk hurriedly past the many autograph books thrust into their faces. Bryan's teddy-bear image and worried smile were a delight to the crowds. Even when feeling exhausted, he would go through the daily ritual of signing as many books as he could with incredible patience, even for a girl whose book he knows he has signed several times before. Bryan says that most fans were polite but some were not. 'If they said, "You look a lot fatter than you do on the telly", for example, I always tried hard not to be rude back.'

11

Heart Attack

Shock as *Street*'s Alf collapses in studio.
The People *newspaper (8 January 1995)*

Like many other stressful experiences in Bryan's life, most of the daunting memories of his first heart attack in the winter of 1991 have been erased or pushed way down inside. The fact that he can remember so little of the incident shows how frightening it was for him, and how determined he is not to relive it, even in his own mind.

For his family, however, the details are still fresh as some of the most terrifying and difficult experiences they have yet had to face. When the one person you are closest to is taken so suddenly and desperately ill, it reminds you of how fragile life really is. Immediate thoughts of how precious they are to you, how much you have taken them for granted, and how frustratingly little you can do to change the situation, flood your mind.

For Norma, the scares about Bryan's health enabled her once again to realize the depths of her own hidden strength as she found the courage and resilience to nurse and support him. This sense of robustness was what had got her through the early days of their marriage together, when there was no money and eight mouths to feed. Now it was here to uphold Bryan at the time he needed it the most.

After yet another long day at the studio, Bryan and Norma had been invited out by their daughter Jacqueline and her husband to share some home-made pizzas. It was a known fact that Bryan did not like pizzas anyway, and will resolutely scrape off the top coating if he has no choice but to eat it. His preferences for dumplings and gravy were not adhered to on this occasion, and he used the excuse to go and sit down in the front room. He was not feeling very much like eating anyway.

Although Norma had known about Bryan's refusal to enjoy pizzas for some time, she had noticed that something had been different about Bryan that day. His time at the studio seemed to have made him unusually irritable, and for several days he had arrived home particularly exhausted, complaining of chronic stomach ache. 'After about five minutes of eating our food, I told Jacqueline that I had been worried about her Dad, and decided that I would just pop in to the front room and see if he was all right. I was quite cautious, as I know that Bryan hates a fuss, but I was feeling very uneasy, and wanted to put my mind at rest. When I got to the room where he was, I knew immediately that something was wrong. He looked very ill as he sat there. I can't describe it. He just looked so pale and was obviously in a lot of distress.'

Norma called out to Jacqueline, who came rushing in, and they decided between them that they should call an ambulance. Bryan refused, and said that he would be absolutely fine, he just needed a lie down. Helping him into the car, Jacqueline drove her parents speedily home, and Bryan managed to shuffle into his house before collapsing into a chair, looking and feeling even worse, with a severe pain around his left shoulder.

A quick exchange of views between mother and daughter, and they decided to call out his local doctor. The GP arrived soon afterwards and, after doing some initial tests, made an immediate decision to admit Bryan, and asked to use the tele-phone to call an ambulance. In /the meantime, he gave his patient an injection of morphine, a drug quite specific in relieving the pain associated with heart failure. It also had a calming effect on Bryan while he waited for the ambulance. The main concern was that the heart attack would not lead to a full cardiac arrest.

Norma joined Bryan in the ambulance, which took them to the local accident and emergency department at Bradford Royal Infirmary about three miles from their home. After seeing her husband whisked off into the emergency ward, the seriousness of the situation began to dawn on Norma. 'I had been quite scared, but these feelings are often pushed aside when you are in the middle of an emergency.' Bryan was promptly stabilized by the medical team with a complex mixture of drugs, drips and oxygen, and Norma was told to go home, as there was nothing more she could do at this time. 'I arrived home at about 2 a.m. and just collapsed into bed. I didn't think I would be able to sleep, but thankfully I did.'

The following morning the full extent of Bryan's diagnosis was revealed by the specialists. Bryan had suffered a heart attack when the left ventricle had come under too much pres-sure, overloaded itself and was forced to slow down. 'I was told that the actual heart attack had probably happened while we were eating our pizzas, and that by the time we got him into hospital it was basically all over. He is a strong man, and this is one of the reasons why his body survived the trauma, but it was a warning to us.

'I was told that he would be kept in hospital for a few weeks to make sure his heart was properly settled, and that with the help of drugs and the right sort of diet, he should be able to make a full recovery. I was just grateful that he was looking so much better, but I never really allowed myself to consider that I might have lost him. That would have been too painful to contemplate.'

Norma did her own research on ischemic heart disease, which had become the most common cause of death in adult Britons, with many factors being blamed, she discovered. Smoking, stress, lack of exercise and obesity are all supposed to predispose towards heart disease. Heart disease can lead to heart failure. But once the heart's inability to pump the blood properly is brought under control by medication, complete bed-rest is the only real way to recovery. Norma knew that the thought of bed-rest would be very depressing for Bryan. He had always been an active man, and all the fighting, stunt work and travelling he had done over the years had given him the expectation that he would always enjoy good health. True, he appreciated his food, and diets had been suggested from time to time, but Bryan was aware that the character of Alf held him to ransom in some ways, even commenting to a friend one day that 'If I lose weight, I lose parts.' An inability to accept himself and his performances as satisfactory would always lead him to push himself further. 'Satisfied' is not a word in Bryan's professional dictionary, and he is never really at peace with any of his performances, which is probably one reason why they are so good.

His frustration at being bed-ridden slowly bubbled inside him, and he was often not the most affable patient on the ward. He detested the hospital food, and was very keen to get back to Norma's home-cooked delicacies. This determination and drive, combined with the sharp focus of getting back home as quickly as possible, served to speed up his recovery. Over the weeks, Bryan made a steady recovery, although this was often hampered by his celebrity status. Situated at the end of the ward, away from the glare of inquisitive eyes, he was still woken up in his bed one time by someone asking for his autograph – a sad example of how some people see television personalities as pieces of public property rather than real people.

The press also hounded him. The hospital, which was inexperienced in such matters, found it difficult to protect Bryan from the persistent demands of the media to know what was really going on. Bryan's condition had been further complicated by the addition of a chest infection, and there was media speculation that this was just a cover for the reality that his health was deteriorating rapidly. They were desperate for the story. Despite a nurse being especially appointed to keep Bryan away from the intrusion of the flash-bulbs, it was impossible for her to keep her eyes on him 24 hours a day. One young press reporter even entered the ward on the pretext of visiting another patient. Carrying a flash-camera hidden among a huge bunch of flowers, he even had the nerve to ask the sickly Bryan some questions before he was discovered by the nursing staff and escorted smartly outside. It is rumoured that in the early days of his hospitalization, the friends and family of other patients in the same ward were made offers for an exclusive picture of 'Alf' in hospital. All refused, but the story made the front pages of many of the tabloids, and running comments on his progress were included in editorials for many weeks to come.

No one had been prepared for the public's response when the news of Bryan's hospitalization broke. 'I think more than 30 bouquets of flowers arrived on the first day, and literally hundreds of cards. I was completely overwhelmed, particularly by the messages saying that people were praying for me.'

As Bryan slowly recovered, the press were allowed in from time to time under the watchful eye of both the hospital authorities and Granada Television. They were anxious to show their support for Bryan while enjoying the extra publicity for the show that this scenario would bring. It was also arranged that Barbara Windsor should make a visit to see Bryan, complete with a *Sun* newspaper reporter and photographer. Bryan could not understand this, as she had never been a close friend of his, and sadly wondered if her publicity office had made the appointment on her behalf.

In the light of recent events, Norma decided that she now had as good a case as any to ask Bryan to leave his television career behind and take things a little easier. 'I had been asking him for some while to consider retirement. He had been working so hard recently, sometimes with a schedule that demanded that he work 16 days in a row without any time off. As he was getting towards 65, and we had all the money we needed, I felt it was the perfect time.'

With a classic rags-to-riches story behind them, Norma and Bryan had saved enough money so that the rest of their lives would be comfortable but not extravagant. Their closest friends agree that they don't live like movie stars. 'One of the most attractive things about them is their ability to serve up baked beans on toast one day and dumplings the next,' say Derek and Margaret Forbes. 'We live just around the corner from them in Shipley, and we always feel we are welcome to pop in, but we never abuse their friendship. It's just as important for us to give as to receive.' Derek and Margaret were able to help in a very practical way as Bryan finally prepared to leave hospital. Derek became an excellent 'taxi driver' for Bryan, who was not allowed to drive for some while after his illness. Margaret was a strong moral support for Norma.

Friendships were an important element in keeping both the ailing Bryan and the tired Norma from fading into their own problems. They had always enjoyed an enormous circle of friends which included those from both in and out of the business, and now spent much more of their spare time entertaining and attending dinner parties.

Friends on the *Street* were just as complimentary about Bryan's and Norma's use of their money. This included Darren Little, Archivist and part of the series management team. Darren's job is to make sure that the many script-writers stay faithful to each character's history and personality. There are anything up to 10 script-writers working on the series at any one time, so it's a big job. Darren got to know Bryan well over the years of working with him on the *Street* and said that he had always found Bryan a very generous person. 'After the birth of my first child, Bryan and Norma kindly gave us the use of their holiday caravan in Yorkshire at a time when we couldn't afford a holiday. It gave us a much-needed break.'

However, even his friends could not persuade Bryan to make the break from that which was most dear to him. Bryan understood his wife's concerns, and many discussions later she reluctantly agreed to let him return. Bryan had been deeply worried for some time that because of his illness the studio may decide not to ask him back anyway. His fear of being dumped so cruelly was increased by the knowledge of the difficulties that his sudden departure had caused. The fact that the producers had to scrap nearly a week's worth of filming and charge the writers with the complex business of rewording the recorded story overnight without Bryan was of great concern to him. All his colleagues would be involved in the arduous task of having to re-learn new lines, re-record new scenes, and some may even have had nights out with their family and friends cancelled because of it. Bryan felt less and less as if he would ever be welcomed back.

The studio bosses had other ideas, though. Whilst sympathizing with Bryan's illness, they realized that the recent publicity surrounding him could only be of help to the series, and they were consequently unwilling even to consider writing Bryan out of the show. On his imminent return, Bryan pointed out the proposed punishing schedule to Granada, who quickly ordered their writers and producers to reduce Alf's appearances. Despite a hurried easing of the recording schedule, however, and an open concern for Bryan's health, little seemed to change quickly enough for Bryan. The flattering, yet unfortunate result of this was that in his first week back Bryan seemed to be working harder than before. 'I'm sure that this situation was not really deliberate,' explains Norma. 'It's just one of those things that was somehow overlooked at the time.'

Bryan's concern to get back to his old way of working probably encouraged him to underplay the effect that his bad health was having on him, and possibly he returned to work too soon. His concern to continue to help others less fortunate than himself was also a contributing factor to him overworking.

He had recently received an Honorary MA given to him for his services to Film, Television and Charity by Bradford University. 'I was doing too much charity work at the time. They spend six months or more getting a fête together, and it means so much to them that you don't feel you can let them down. I would end up travelling all over the place, really wearing myself down and leaving my family behind. I felt obliged to attend charity functions because of my celebrity status, and that this was expected of me. I genuinely wanted to help as many people as often as I could, but eventually it all got on top of me. The great comic Les Dawson said once that you could spend every moment of the day appearing at charity events, so that you wouldn't have any time to pursue your own career. Then when you are not on the box any more, nobody will want you. Suddenly I discovered this amazing magic word called "No", and that's what I use a lot these days. I think it's important to do charity work, but it must be in balance with the other priorities in your life.'

Other 'extra-curricular' activities had included attending spectacular functions such as the Lord Mayor's Show in London. With Lillie Langtry's Landau cruising past a crowd of half a million lining the streets of London, Bryan and his co-star Sue Nicholls soon found that their arms ached intensely after an hour of waving back at the masses. 'We were dressed in the most wonderful costumes, complete with furry hats,' recalls Sue. It was to become one of the fondest memories she would keep of working with Bryan. 'It was special because it was just the two of us,' she explains. 'We had been working on the *Street* as a screen couple for more than 10 years, and that has been like a marriage in its own way. As we sat in the open-topped coach and paraded through the streets of London, we recognized it as a moment that only the two of us would share.'

Their only regret over the event is that it was never recorded nor used for the *Street* storyline in any way, and particularly as Alf had become Mayor of Weatherfield by then, it seemed like a sadly missed opportunity. Indeed, both even expressed hurt that this unique event had not been used more effectively by the *Street*. As they arrived at their destination and alighted – into the arms of their respective 'real-life' spouses, they consoled themselves that this had been a precious moment just for them.

The grand banquet that followed at the Guildhall, hosted by the Mayor and the then Prime Minister John Major, seemed to ease the pain somewhat. Bryan relaxed in the glitz and glamour and was no stranger to Number 10 itself, for the previous Prime Minister, Mrs Thatcher, had visited Alf's corner shop and invited Bryan and Norma to visit her London home during her last term in office. Bryan was very amused when it seemed that many of those he was rubbing shoulders with at Number 10 were from the opposition Labour Party.

Bryan's workload in and out of the studio continued to increase as his health improved, but it is little wonder that less than four years after his initial heart problems Bryan was taken ill once again. This time it was while filming in the studio itself. *The People* newspaper of 8 January 1995 records that '*Coronation Street* star Bryan Mosley has been rushed to hospital after nearly collapsing on set … the shocked cast heard him complain of dizzy spells and feeling unwell during filming … one of the production staff said everyone was very worried about Bryan…'

This time Bryan was given the unusual opportunity to allay the worst of fears by telephoning the press himself the next day and making a personal statement. '*Street* star Bryan is laughing off health rumours,' announced the leader in *The People*. '*Coronation Street* star Bryan Mosley today hit back at rumours about his health and told his fans: "I'm fit and well … I have been inundated with telephone calls from people concerned about my health, but I thank them for their wishes and am pleased to say that I am fine. It was a routine check at the hospital. I do not know how these rumours start, but I am glad to say it was not true."' In reply to the previous newspaper comments on how ironic it was that his character Alf had been forced to give up work and sell the corner shop after suffering a heart attack, he notes, 'People sometimes get mixed up with what happens on the screen, but I am fit and well and back at work.'

The truth is that Bryan had genuinely been feeling unwell at work, but this time had arranged to see a doctor for himself.

Ironically, his screen 'wife' had persuaded Alf to go on a strict diet, and Bryan himself was forced to reconsider his own doctor's advice about his food intake – advice he had previously ignored. 'This funny little turn made me start to take his advice seriously, and I began to look at all the diets which would help my heart.'

The fact that Bryan also had a chronic form of diabetes, discovered only a few years previously, complicated the matter of diet. It was a concern of the doctors to balance both conditions, since the equilibrium could be easily upset, which could cause Bryan further difficulties.

For a while life seemed to settle into the old way of things. Bryan was glad to be firmly established back at the *Street*, and Norma packed the bags, accompanying Bryan between their Shipley home and their Manchester flat, according to whatever the recording schedule would dictate.

Life as normal also meant holidays. They share a love of travelling and have been to most places around the world, sometimes with one of the major cruise lines, who provide television stars the opportunity to travel with them as a celebrity perk, but mostly to secret destinations with as little planning as possible.

'The opportunity for me to travel with Norma was like my boyhood dreams coming true. I had always wanted to go to Rome or Mexico, and be part of history. Seeing these amazing places has the effect of making me feel quite small and helpless in a busy, noisy world.'

Spectacular locations are not always high on the agenda. On their twenty-fifth wedding anniversary, Bryan suggested that they should visit India and the Taj Mahal, but Norma wanted to re-live their honeymoon days on the river boat. Happily, they did this with greater success than they had the first time around!

Bryan never went abroad until he was 35. Their first holiday cost as many pounds as his age, an amount they could not really afford. Nevertheless, the trip to Venice was worth all their hard savings. Bryan has clear memories of places around the world which hold a special significance for him, including a second trip to the city of water. 'One of the oldest palaces in Venice is now a hotel overlooking the Grand Canal. We stayed there for three or four days, accompanied by our friends, Ted and Flo Heeley. We had to go up the golden staircase, which has traces of fifteenth-century gold leaf. Then we had to cross a superb ante-room to our own private stairs. We laughingly call it the "'Otel 'Ow Much?"'

Holidays with the children had often taken place in an enormous tent which would take Bryan hours to erect. A later addition to the family was the purchase of a very dilapidated caravan near Filey. It was rusty and sometimes leaked when it rained. Bryan still looks back on those simple days of fun and laughter with great affection. Now that he has replaced the tent with a cruise ship, and the caravan with an aeroplane, every opportunity for a holiday is relished. 'We have toiled up Chichen Itza Pyramid and into the "lost" city of Palenque in the Mexican jungle, narrowly missing one of the deadliest snakes, a beautiful green mamba which suddenly crossed our path. We climbed into the King's Chamber in the Great Pyramid at Giza in Egypt and travelled up the Nile to Luxor and Abu Simbel. In short, we have been blessed with some marvellous memories.'

Now a different set of travelling arrangements had been put upon Norma, as she had recently been nursing her own mother and had been regularly journeying to Leeds to be with her. Nora had been ill for some time, and Norma was dedicated to looking after her mother, but the constant to-ing and fro-ing between the two cities and the worry of leaving Bryan on his own for too long had exhausted her. When her mother's sad death finally came in late winter, Norma was certainly in need of a break and suggested to Bryan that they should spend a week in Portugal. They had planned to go to Disneyland with the children and grandchildren, but Bryan had to pull out, so they went by themselves.

Norma planned a holiday which would take them to the beautiful coast of Lanzarote. A few days away from it all would be a gateway of opportunity to relax and take things easy, and recover from the trauma of the last few months. What lay ahead was the gateway to something else for which neither of them were prepared.

12

The Relic

'I'm a living miracle!'
Bryan Mosley (July 1998)

Nearing the end of their holiday break, Norma and Bryan really felt that the past had been put well and truly behind them. It was whilst they began to pack their bags for the journey home that Bryan started to complain of feeling ill once more. He recognized the symptoms, but refused to acknowledge what they might mean, since he was loath to face the thought that his heart was under stress once more.

Whilst Norma gathered up their belongings Bryan sat and quietly looked out at the view and prayed that God would be with him. He acknowledged how frightened he was and allowed his mind to wander to those moments of loneliness in hospital five years before, when his faith had been such a comfort to him whilst in the isolation of the ward. There had been a real sense in which God had been right there with him, in such a tangible way that he could almost reach out and touch him. As he prayed now, there was once again that same sense of peace and calm which had surrounded him before. He relaxed and even started to feel better.

Awaiting the call to board the flight out of Lanzarote Airport, Norma tried to arrange a seat which would give Bryan

166

some extra leg space. This was not to be. The cabin was extremely congested and the lack of leg room meant that Bryan's knees were hunched up all the way home, with little room to move for nearly three hours. She feared the extra strain that this would put on his heart as it battled to pump the blood round restricted limbs.

Bryan found the journey generally uncomfortable, but remained calm and relaxed throughout the flight. He was relieved when they landed safely back on home soil. Eventually arriving back at their house, Bryan fell into his favourite chair by the window once more, and was obviously exhausted. Plenty of rest over the weekend brought Bryan a renewed sense of vigour, and he was eager to get back to the *Street* first thing on Monday morning. Even as he went through the gates of the studio, he could sense that all was not well, but he struggled through the day and arrived back home at the Manchester flat that they had bought some years earlier, looking pale and weary.

'I'll be OK,' he said. 'I've just got a few more scenes to do, then in a couple of days I can take it easy again.' Norma was not convinced by Bryan's bravado. Never one to push her husband, she had always allowed him to make decisions for himself, and contented herself with the thought that he was the only one who truly knew how he felt.

As Bryan stared out of the window at the boats moving down the canal, he began to feel worse and worse. A welcome cup of tea from Norma brought some comfort but could not erase the growing realization of what was happening within. Then, as he grappled with the thoughts of letting his colleagues down once again, with scripts being rewritten and rehearsed overnight to cover for his absence, mixed with the fear of what was happening to him, he eventually accepted the reality of the situation and, leaning forward, quietly asked Norma to call an ambulance.

'I could see that Bryan was becoming more and more distressed, and whilst waiting for the ambulance I was worried for his safety, and felt absolutely helpless,' Norma recalls. 'It was the feeling of breathlessness that was the most frightening. I could see that it was becoming increasingly difficult for him to catch his breath, even though he was sitting perfectly still. He described the feeling as if he was slowly drowning, and he was obviously terrified.'

The ambulance arrived in a heavy snowstorm and this time they were taken to Hope Hospital in Manchester, where the doctors once again stabilized his heart with drugs. They noted how the left ventricle had blown up like a balloon, and congestion in the heart had caused water to build up in his lungs. He really had been drowning, and he felt that it was a miracle that he had survived another attack. Drugs were administered to thin his blood and so enable the damaged heart to pump with less strain, and Bryan relaxed back into the care of the hospital staff once more.

After a few days of seeing that Bryan was in safe hands, Norma thought it best to make the journey back home to Shipley for a while. This would at least enable her to do some washing, check on the house and bring some fresh clothes back to Manchester. The doctors realized that she had not grasped the severity of the attack and persuaded her against leaving the city. 'I suppose I just hadn't taken it all in. I mean, it was just like a repeat of the other times when we had a scare, but everything was all right in the end, and I expected it to be so again. Once the doctors told me how critical he was, I decided that going home to collect fresh clothes was not really a priority any more. I just went back to the flat and cried.'

The type of condition and the age of the patient dictated that an operation was not appropriate and complete bed-rest was once again prescribed – this time for a much longer period, and without the intrusion of the press. This protection from the media was helped by the fact that the hospital provided their star guest with a room all to himself. The problem for Bryan was that there was no television to watch. The problem for Norma was that the room seemed filthy, depressing and bleak. It was hardly the right atmosphere for recovery for a man who is used to his home comforts, she considered. After one day of sitting together whilst Bryan mused over a cross-word and Norma contemplated a word puzzle, it became too much for her. She would do something to brighten up his room herself. 'I got so fed up with leaving Bryan in that stuffy, isolated room which reminded you of all the worst things about hospitals. He looked so miserable every time I left, I would cry all the way home.'

She was up so eagerly the next morning with her game-plan that the shops were not even open. 'I stood outside our local electrical shop and waited for nine o'clock to arrive. The shop-keeper was most surprised to see me, and I left with a smart portable TV which I knew would bring the colour back to Bryan's face.' Returning to the hospital, Norma took her prize out of its box and placed it on a table in front of Bryan, and switched it on. Bryan's face lit up simultaneously as the television burst into colour.

Setting about covering the chipped and peeling walls with the many cards sent in by well-wishers and friends, she placed a small Bible text in the centre of the wall, that she hoped would encourage him. The cardboard box which had contained the TV was also put to good use – it was turned on its back, covered with a small cloth, and used as a coffee table. Norma left Bryan that night filled with a sense of satisfaction and renewed hope.

The cards on the wall were a constant reminder of just how much Bryan was being missed by the 15 million television viewers before whom he was so used to appearing each week. Even the newsgroups and forums of the country's latest toy, the Internet, were buzzing with the story of Alf's sad situation. There are more than a dozen Websites run by dedicated *Coronation Street* fans the world over, from the USA to Canada. Most are operated by fans in the UK providing instantly available information on the series to anyone with a personal computer and a modem. The sites contain constantly reviewed story-line updates, character assessments, backstage news and gossip, and even maps of the houses in the Street, alongside lists of all the fan club addresses world-wide.

The sad news that Bryan was back in hospital was flashed across the world via the Internet. As Mike Plowman from the *Coronation Street* Visual Update Website commented, 'Obviously, Bryan's illness and absence from the show had been widely discussed amongst the CS net newsgroup, and I received many, many emails from people all around the world who wanted to see him back at work.'

Bryan says, 'It was wonderful to receive so many messages from people wanting to see me back on the *Street*. The staff at the hospital were marvellous too. Clive Nultey was a night nurse who was a great source of hope and encouragement to me. Lying there all alone, feeling so ill and wondering if I was going to make it through the night, I often thought, "Bryan, your time's up, mate!" Clive would see me dispirited, and, sitting beside me in the darkness, would gently and confidently tell me I was going to be OK. He was like a visiting angel to me. I felt totally surrounded by love and affection in the hospital, and I'm sure it had a positive effect on my recovery.'

Over the next few weeks, Bryan made excellent progress and was sent home earlier than expected, since the doctors believed that it would speed up the healing process if he was surrounded with his own comforts. He was still struggling with his breathing and had found that sitting up in the hospital bed had enabled him to breathe more easily, and more importantly, it had reduced his fear that he might suffocate. He even slept in the special chair that the hospital had brought him, and he was to continue this practice for more than a year.

Still extremely breathless, Bryan had oxygen cylinders connected to a face mask which he could place over his mouth to help him breathe properly. Spare cylinders were kept at home and at his flat in Manchester. He also had a machine which would exercise his lungs by causing them to retract automatically. 'We've seen the funny side of all this too,' Bryan says. 'One night I coughed and Norma said, "Oh, you're still alive, then!"'

The daily dose of six different pills which looked so tiny and ineffectual when held in his palm, but which had such an effect when swallowed, added an important focus to his daily routine, and reminded him of the seriousness of his condition. He also made regular visits to the hospital for monitoring and eventually received a special course of drugs. 'The real trouble was anaemia, through lack of quality blood. A new treatment which helps to create red corpuscles in the spine is called EPO, and they give it to people on dialysis. It's a bit like a massive infusion of iron. I go in looking like I'm all yellow and ill, I have this injection, and come out looking fantastic.'

One of the complications in Bryan's condition was the fact that he had been a diabetic for some while, and this was to plague him with several bouts of temporary blindness. 'I think diabetes is the most insidious, evil and treacherous disease there is. It is possible that I always had the condition, but it was only discovered later in my life. It was a very hot summer in 1976, and I was drinking an enormous amount of liquid but still feeling thirsty. I went to a homeopath, who said that he suspected I had diabetes, and that I had better go and see a doctor. This I did, and he diagnosed me immediately, and put me on a strict diet.'

The Diabetes UK Website explains that:

Diabetes can occur at any age. It is a health problem that seems to be becoming more common. There are nearly 1.5 million people in the UK today with diabetes, with another estimated 1 million people who may have diabetes without knowing it. Although diabetes cannot yet be cured, it can be treated very successfully, and this allows most people to work, travel and lead an active life just as they did before. Currently, there is no cure for diabetes, but the good news is that the disease can be managed. People with diabetes can live rich, happy lives.

Diabetes is one of very few illnesses where an understanding of the condition together with constant self-monitoring are the keys to good control. This control is the responsibility of the patient. Self-care is more than important, it is essential. Good blood glucose control – that is, keeping BG levels as well controlled as possible, and very similar to those in someone who does not have diabetes – is the key to minimizing the likelihood of complications later on.

Bryan admits that his own sense of 'self-care' was not very good. 'I hate all the fuss of diets and what to eat and what not to eat, but I was too stupid to take my doctor's advice seriously.

He told me to lose weight as well, and control my diet, but I couldn't do it properly, and in the end I gave up trying.'

Dropsy, or oedema, was also diagnosed, and Bryan's ankles would swell up due to congestion with an excess of retained tissue fluid. This excess water is normally removed by the circulation of the blood and the kidneys, so disease of either characteristically results in such a condition. It can cause all manner of complications and is an essential part of the treatment of chronic heart failure. It also added to Bryan's burdens.

Sitting in the area at the bottom of their garden where Norma had organized the erection of a small net awning, Bryan would contemplate his future. 'I had a lot of time to think about things. Quite a privilege in some ways. I did find myself rejoicing in the wonderful pattern that my life had taken. Being ill was a real nuisance and very painful at times, as I was very frustrated at not being able to get back to work. However, I was also able to reflect on how much God still loved me. The incredible love and care demonstrated by my family clearly showed me how much gratitude I should have. The most precious was the love shown to me by my dear wife, Norma.'

Bryan thought he might lose Norma when she was diagnosed with cancer 14 years previously. He had wept and prayed every moment that God would spare her. His prayers were answered, and they had enjoyed many wonderful years since. 'I could see God's love in her even though she suffered a great deal emotionally because of the trauma. I watched her nurse her own mother in her last illness, and Norma's tenderness was a blazing example to me. Then I became ill and her love for me was demonstrated in her concern and care.

'I remembered how, when I was very low-spirited in hospital, she came every day to be with me. One day, to my delight, she brought one of my grandchildren along with my daughters Jacqueline and Simone. I had thought at one stage that I would never see my grandchildren again. Charlotte, Roseanna, Tom and Lauren call me 'Pappos'. They got me into a wheelchair and took me on a whirlwind tour of the hospital with the little one on my knee! Never had the air tasted fresher, and their exuberance had given me the courage to go on.'

A starry summer night brought Bryan's wandering thoughts to focus on the greatness of God. Standing alone in the darkness, he gazed up, and it struck him that God was truly awesome. He had recently read that astronomers had focused on an area of the sky the size of a grain of sand, and discovered billions of stars and galaxies that dwarf our own Milky Way. He would enjoy memorizing verses in the Bible that would bring him comfort, and started to run what he could remember of Psalm 139 through his mind:

> Where can I escape from you? Where could I get away from your presence? If I went up to Heaven you would be there; if I lay down in the world of the dead, you would be there. If I flew away beyond the east or lived in the farthest place in the west you would be there to lead me, you would be there to help me. I could ask the darkness to hide me or the light round me to turn into night, but even darkness is not dark for you, and the night is as bright as the day. Darkness and light are the same to you.

Bryan thought to himself, 'God is everywhere. The Pantheists who see God in everything are somehow missing the point. God's Spirit is also there, even closer than they imagine. So I put myself in God's hands and gain strength and hope from him.' Comforted by these thoughts, Bryan took in a lungful of warm night air, and retired to bed.

As the long, hot summer of 1997 wore on, it seemed as if the sun had never received any instructions to go to bed, and the lace curtains of the awning where Bryan sat each day created a strong pattern of dappled sunlight on the walls. As he got slowly better, he even began to be able to sit in the direct sunlight, and loved soaking up the sun, very soon becoming as brown as a berry. The effect of this was quite odd, because even when he felt really under par, he looked extremely healthy to everyone else. This enforced inactivity had its negative effect too, and slowly it began to underline Bryan's enormous irritation at not being able to work. 'I found it so very frustrating being ill and not able to do what I would do normally. I'm usually a very active person and in the end I just got very angry, not really at God or anyone else, but at the circumstances I was in. I really felt for Norma, who had to carry me about, and nurse me, but there is the proof of real love being shown. Not in words but in action. I also received a lot of support from many people, and I was very grateful to them, but the only thing I could think about was to get better, and get on with my life again.'

After several weeks Norma recognized the beginning of a slow, downward spiral into depression. 'It was really the sitting around all day that annoyed him, and when the summer started to fade, so did his spirits. He desperately wanted to be better quickly, and the speed with which he was making good recovery just did not seem fast enough for him. Nothing seemed to be able to brighten him up. He would just give a groan if I asked him if he would like a cup of tea or let him know that dinner was ready. It seemed as if he had totally given up on life, and it started to get me down too. After six months at home, I realized that what he needed was a breath of fresh air, a change of scenery. In fact it was what we both needed.

My mother had left me some money, so I decided to use this to make a pilgrimage to Lourdes. Not for any reason in particular, except that I'd always wanted to go, and I thought it would be a great trip for Bryan.'

When she asked Bryan if he would like to go, he said he would at first, but then kept changing his mind. He did this on a daily basis, as if he was stalling it all the time. Norma knew he would not be allowed to go by plane, as the pressure could cause problems for his heart. The only way was to drive, but this would be a 3,000-mile round trip, and she wondered whether, in his state, it would be possible. The other major hurdle to overcome was that Norma had never learnt to drive, and she would not allow Bryan to drive either. Anyway, such a long and arduous journey would need the support of someone else. Norma considered some friends they knew, and wondered which one to call. She was very nervous about asking such a huge favour of anyone, but then she remembered Peter Byrne. He had been a good friend of the family for some years, and was the greengrocer who had paid Bryan's wages in carrots and potatoes many years before. He had also been a driver for the 'Jumbulances' organization which arranges to take pilgrims and their sick relatives down to the revered grotto in the south of France.

Peter readily accepted the request, but agreed with Norma that a Jumbulance trip might not be in Bryan's best interests. He would most certainly find it very difficult to relax surrounded by a group of people, all asking him questions about Alf. It was finally decided that Peter would drive them solo, in their own car, the whole distance. They would make no forward arrangements for accommodation, they would take each day as it came, but they would anticipate that the whole journey would take about 10 days. They also elected to leave as soon as possible.

However, Bryan kept on making excuses not to go. Every time Peter suggested a day, Bryan would change his mind. In the end Peter asked him one morning if he wanted to go, and came straight round before he changed his mind! Peter stuffed Bryan into the front seat whilst Norma climbed into the back. On their first day they managed to drive from Yorkshire, straight under the Channel Tunnel, though Norma was a little hesitant about this. She said nothing, but Bryan sensed that she felt claustrophobic until they reached the other end. Able to arrive in Calais before it was too dark, they started to look for somewhere to eat and stay overnight. Bryan is wonderfully impatient, particularly in restaurants, where he will leave if he is not served within a few minutes of being seated. They had no time to waste and found a little tourist hotel near the centre of the town, getting an early night in readiness for the long journey to follow.

Croissants and coffee set the mood for the threesome, who made an early start the next morning. The countryside which constantly sped by gave the pilgrims a taste of freedom and escape, which brought an atmosphere of hopefulness to the task ahead. The fact that none of them could speak French only heightened their sense of adventure, although they were constantly aware of just how ill Bryan was. The long hours were filled with every song they could remember from 'Knees up Mother Brown' to 'Great is thy faithfulness'. Peter would ask Norma what the name of a particular woman in a particular film was, and whilst Norma was still trying to think, Bryan would come in with the answer. 'He has an incredible memory for films,' she says. Regular stops along the way ensured that the patient's circulation remained lively and the driver's alertness remained active.

On this journey Bryan suffered with car sickness. 'It was really strange,' says Norma, 'because usually I am the one who gets travel sick, and normally I have to sit in the front seat with the window open to try and retain my composure. Somehow, Bryan feeling sick helped me to focus on his suffering instead of my own.'

Not that she was comfortable. 'I was in the back seat, sandwiched between an oxygen cylinder on one side and a cool-box full of medication on the other. Peter had also brought a fan with him, which was useful to rest my arm on, but whenever we went too fast round a corner I felt I was going to be crushed. The cool-box was packed to capacity with diabetic syringes and Bryan's tablets which all had to be kept cool. I prevented myself from moaning too much by reminding myself that a pilgrimage was not supposed to be comfortable but a sacrifice anyway.'

Norma recalls how one of their stops involved visiting a small hospital run by nuns for sick and handicapped people in a local village alongside the main road south. 'Peter took me inside and introduced me to the Sisters nursing the many sick and dying people trying to reach Lourdes in the hope of finding healing and spiritual refreshment. He told me that it was unlikely that many of them would actually make it. It suddenly dawned on me that he was also talking about Bryan. We both wept as we considered the very real possibility that we might be coming home without Bryan.'

After four days the exhausted travellers had almost reached their destination, but had decided to stop overnight in a little guest-house some distance away, so that they could make proper arrangements for accommodation in Lourdes itself. They wanted to make sure they were staying as near to the shrine as possible, so that they could get down there first thing after breakfast.

Managing to book the last two rooms in an hotel within walking distance of the grotto, it turned out that the constant rain that had dogged their journey suddenly became a blessing. The area around the shrine was not at all crowded and they joined the very small queue of people who were already there, slowly entering the grotto soon afterwards. For Norma this was a real answer to prayer, as she wasn't sure for how long Bryan would have been able to stand. Peter had arranged a wheelchair for Bryan to use, but he had firmly refused.

The history behind the grotto had begun on Thursday 11 February 1858. At Massabielle Grotto, a 'lady dressed in white', believed to be the Virgin Mary, was reported to have appeared to Bernadette Soubirous for the first time. Seventeen more such apparitions followed. Nearly a century and a half later, 5 million pilgrims and visitors come to Lourdes each year to bow their heads in prayer in the very place where Mary appeared. The silent, personal prayers spoken by Norma and Bryan focused on their commitment to God, their commitment to each other, and their anxieties over Bryan's health. Emerging into the daylight once more, they realized that they had not drunk the water, an important spiritually symbolic aspect of the visit. Peter and Norma left Bryan sitting on a wooden bench as they re-entered the grotto, returning quickly with a cup which they then passed to one another, sipping at the contents in turn. The tension of the journey, the fears of whether they would ever arrive, the anxiety of Bryan's condition, and the acute sense of being in the presence of God suddenly erupted amongst the three of them in a cascade of tears. In those moments pain and joy were companions. Yet if one imagines that Lourdes is a place of sickness and sadness, you would be mistaken. It is a place of great joy, great laughter, and above all, great hope.

At this moment Norma noticed an immediate and remarkable change in her husband. 'It wasn't a physical change but a mental and spiritual one. Whilst he had been holding on to his illness, he had been trying to work it all out, even feeling accountable for all that had happened, and holding himself answerable for his own recovery. I think he was tormented by worry, but of course he never let it show it on the outside. Now he could just let go of all these pent-up feelings. It was as if he was finally able to say to God, "It's out of my hands now. I can't carry this any more. It's up to you." It was a great release for him.'

The journey home the next day seemed to have a renewed sense of energy and expectancy all of its own, with Bryan himself declaring that the pilgrimage had been one of the most significant times in his life. In fact it had been life-changing. Having sat and wept at Lourdes, Bryan realized that the long climb to healing had begun. He accepted that he was totally helpless on his own, and the vigour that he had been given was, for now, depleted. Now was the time to let go, and just as he had relied on their dear friend Peter to make the very real sacrifice of driving them all that way, he was now concerned to rely on God to carry him onto the next part of his life's journey. He had been tempted to give in to despair, but through the love of his companions he had come to realize that he had a new life and that he should not be ruled by his fears any more. He also found that he could trust in God in a new way, and not look too deeply for answers to his problems. Surprised to discover how liberating this was, he was now determined to use his energies and gifts to try to love others as he would like to be loved.

For Norma too, the pilgrimage had been a source of great strength. Norma, the one who was always so graceful and gentle, had become enormously drained with all the recent pressure of Bryan's illness and everything associated with it. The trip had given her new momentum, and fresh vigour.

Many people on pilgrimages bring back a relic of the site they have visited as a reminder of what they have seen, and what touched them. It is a reflection of his dry sense of humour that, instead of a stone or a cross or a picture, Bryan had bought a duck. Peter had seen this 'relic' sitting amongst all the statues and holy pictures that he considered 'tat'. 'They even had "blinking" Jesus pictures with eyes that would open and close as you went past, but the duck made me cry with laughter.' It was a well-beaked bird dressed in a bright-yellow sou'wester with matching hat and wellington boots. 'It was somehow quite appropriate because it rained so much,' laughs Bryan. 'It even squirts water and croons "Singing in the Rain"!'

But the duck was not the only thing they brought home. Half-way back, they stopped off to pray just as the rain started to clear. 'It was amazing because when we got out of the car the rain stopped, the sun came out and a beautiful rainbow filled the sky,' recalls Bryan. 'The timing was so much like the ending to a film that it was almost unbelievable.'

As they stepped back in through their front door, they knew that this special memory would last for a very long time. The rainbow symbolized the fact that they had a future with a new sense of hope and promise.

13

Ambition and Faith

He who provides for this life, but
takes no care for eternity, is wise
for a moment, but a fool forever.

John Tillotson

'Feelings are strange things,' reflects Bryan. 'We can be exhilarated with joy one second, and suddenly sunk into gloom at the slightest setback. I see friends with intense problems who, through faith, survive and triumph. Our world is such that despair lurks around every corner, so most people, I think, do not really look at their feelings.' So says the man who has put an enormous amount of feeling and emotion into every character that he has portrayed.

Having grown up in an era when feelings were never really discussed, Bryan was not used to examining his own until fairly recently. It was an offer made to him by his local parish priest to go on a Marriage Encounter weekend that started the ball rolling. 'I said I really didn't think there was anything wrong with my marriage, and I certainly didn't need a whole weekend to work on it, thank you very much! Then I began to think about how much importance I put on my relationship with Norma. Did I really see our marriage as something that I should put time and effort into? After all, I gave my career, my kids, myself plenty of time, so why not give some time to my marriage too? There was always room for improvement anyway, I reasoned. I also mused over the fact that marriages were under such pressure these days, and I supposed it would be true to admit that in that case you need all the help you can get. Anyway, I thought, it's better to do an "MOT" on our marriage now, rather than wait until something happens and it's too late to repair. So, I promised myself that I would go one day, but maybe not just yet. Then there was a spare weekend in my diary which corresponded with the dates of the Marriage Encounter weekend, and so the decision was made for me.'

As they arrived at the beautiful country retreat, any nervousness was calmed by the genuinely warm welcome they received. They were not looked upon as 'stars' either, but were treated in the same way as the other 20 or so couples attending, and this they found very refreshing. 'As we listened to the presenters talking,' recalls Bryan, 'we could see how outside strains put such demands on a marriage that it can quickly become a burden rather than a joy. Time just for one another is easily snatched away, and without being properly tended and watered, the emotional side of a relationship dies and shrivels to become an empty shell. How many times have I seen this happen in the lives of those around me? Suddenly I was determined that this would not happen to me, and I listened intently to all that was being said.

'I was especially moved by the presenting couples' honesty and vulnerability as they shared their own experiences of marriage, and I was eager to have the chance to discuss some of these points with Norma. When we did have a chance to look privately in on our own relationship, I was astounded by all the things we had never talked about before. In more than

25 years of being together, there were things we had always been afraid to bring into the open. The result of talking about these things was a greater understanding and appreciation which deepened our love.

'It certainly turned out to be one of the best weekends we have ever had in terms of getting to know each other. It's amazing how, over the years, you forget what the person you originally married is really like. All the reasons you courted and fell in love are still there, but they've just been covered over by layer upon layer of other responsibilities, burdens, worries and pressures. It was good to get back to basics and rediscover each other, and have time to listen and understand the other's thoughts and feelings too, without any interruptions. I put a lot of the success of our marriage down to Norma. She has been a tremendous support and spiritual guide. She's a wonderful woman and I see her as a gift from God.'

For Bryan it was not only a chance to examine his marriage, but to examine himself as well, although at first he did not really welcome the opportunity to talk about his own feelings. A very private man, even at home, it was not easy for him to share what was going on inside himself. 'I found it difficult to accept my own feelings, particularly the ones I don't like, such as greed and envy. Fear and anger were two emotions which I had also kept firmly locked away all my life. I couldn't believe it when one of the couples started talking about what his own fear felt like. He told us that he had a dread of unknown creatures in the dark whenever he took the dog for a walk. This rang a loud bell in me, and I realized how I spent much time avoiding being frightened.

'The war had surrounded me with people who, I now saw, must have been petrified with fear, grief and seeming hopelessness. They put on a front to encourage others, particularly

their children. Having recognized why I seemed fearless, I had
to begin to deal with it, and this freed me to accept all the bits
I was ashamed of, and I painfully began to address the job of
turning those negatives into good.

'I found I had the ability to face and even accept these feelings, without being overwhelmed by them. Of course, I knew
that I would still be fearful at times. Every time I saw a loved one
I was sadly aware that it may be for the last time, but my hope
was that, as St Thomas More wrote, "We may merrily meet in
heaven." I reflected on what a glorious mystery that was.'

Norma was thrilled by Bryan's discoveries and noted that
his ability to face these emotions and understand them gave
him the capacity to communicate at a much deeper level with
her, with others and with himself. They both returned home
with their love for each other having grown more in that
weekend than in many years of struggling through life
together. 'We were understanding each another better and
accepting each other in a new way. The children could even
see a difference in us, which was very encouraging.
Communication is something that is easily lost between
couples. Society is all about the family unit, and I think it is
vitally important that we uphold this whenever we can.'

They were also invited to get involved in leading some of
the weekends themselves, which they readily accepted, and
gave a lot of input in the Engagement Encounter which, as the
name suggests, helps to prepare young people for their forthcoming life of marriage together. 'We were amazed to be
invited out to Zimbabwe,' says Bryan, 'where we started
Engagement Encounters that have continued ever since. God
is the God of surprises, and we made many dear friends whom
we hope to go back and visit one day. We were even charged by
two lions whilst out on a safari! Fortunately we were all in a

very well-protected bus at the time, but it was still a great thrill. We even had a picnic in the jungle surrounded by iridescent dragonflies, as we watched the sun go down. The next day we stood on the very brink of the mighty Victoria Falls, and I was totally enthralled by the deafening sound of the rushing water and the power that lay behind it. How anyone cannot believe in a creator God when confronted with a sight like that is beyond me.'

Bryan and Norma have made many long-standing friends through the Encounter organization, and as a couple who like to be with others, this brings them much satisfaction. 'One couple we still keep in touch with are Peter and Rosemary. Their son, Duncan, was in England with the Royal Ballet School. We went on holiday in France and, purely by chance, met Christopher Gable, who took the reigns at the Northern Ballet, and Duncan later joined them. My daughter offers accommodation to visiting thespians, and behold, Duncan and his wife stayed with her several times. I really think I have a very large extended family!'

The Encounter organization is Christian-based, but is intended for those from all walks of life and all beliefs. 'You don't have to be a church-goer to attend.' Church-going itself is a regular activity for Bryan, but, 'Going to church is the least important aspect of my faith, because God is interested in every area of my life. I take his presence with me wherever I go. I can pray in my dressing-room, or in the car, or on the set of *Coronation Street*. He's always there. I don't just leave God in church on a Sunday morning. I try to walk with God on a day-to-day basis. It's a journey, after all – a developing relationship, like a rope that becomes thicker and eventually unbreakable.'

He believes that denominations can cause a lot of confusion, and that all the Christian churches share the same basic beliefs

– they just like to worship God in differing ways. 'Everybody has to choose the right one for them. I'm not comfortable worshipping God in a charismatic way, but I'm not against anyone else clapping their hands and dancing around. I feel that the most important aspect of worship is to do what Jesus said and to worship God "in spirit and in truth". So long as you are reaching out for God, that's all that matters. Sometimes I think that rather than announcing victory in our Christian lives, we should be on our knees pleading for mercy.

'One of the most important commandments is to try and love your neighbour as yourself. The little lady who goes in and does the flower arranging is just as important as the pastor who preaches. I think this equality is an important aspect of God's love for us, but it's sad when people in the Church have difficulty in loving each other. Petty squabbles can be and should be avoided. Instead of judging others so much, we need to take a good look at ourselves.'

Bryan himself has encountered Christians who feel that he is obliged to attend their function just because he shares their faith. He is annoyed at this, but thinks forgiveness is another key element of life together. He is, however, adamant in his view that the Church is often too soft. 'The Church in this country is going wrong when it bends over backwards to accommodate people rather than standing its ground on important issues. We are supposed to be setting an example, but often we are so weak and we don't like others disliking us. I chastise myself for not being more active in speaking out on issues I really care about. Abortion is a terrible thing which I am opposed to. I think it is obscene to destroy a life which is God-given, in such an easy and free way. I have also seen so many women torn apart by the guilt of having had an abortion. It makes me so sad to see how they will often carry this

187

guilt for the rest of their lives. Nevertheless, there is total forgiveness from God for a woman who has gone through this – he still loves them. I'm not Mr Perfect, of course, and I hate the way I am sometimes. I do swear, and although it lets the steam out, I am ashamed of it and I try not to. I am comforted by the knowledge that God is still working on me!

'I have, of course, fallen in my faith many times, and still do, but I remind myself that my goal is to try and live as God intends me to live. Fortunately, when we fall, God does not put us all the way back to the beginning, like some children's game of "Ludo". No, he picks us up and we continue our journey, but probably wiser! So, when I fall, I must not lie there in the mud feeling sorry for myself. Nor must I give in to the temptation to give up on my faith. I must carry on. I can rely on God to help me, but he has also given me the means to make my own decisions and choices. I must put in some of my own determination in striving for this goal, knowing that God will guide me when I falter.

'It's so vital to know that we can be forgiven. The Church should be able to reach out into society – not by condemning, though. Christ never condemned, but he did say, "Go and sin no more." You've done it, be forgiven, but now get on with the rest of your life.

'That's why Christ died on the cross. If everyone embraced a belief in God, and understood how much he loved them, the world would change overnight. Of course, it won't happen, because people say they can't believe, they won't believe, they don't want to believe, it's too difficult to believe, they can't understand it, so therefore they can't do it. It's amazing what excuses people will come up with to avoid God. Some people think that to have a faith would put a lot of restrictions on them, but I challenge people to investigate for themselves rather than just not bothering. He's only a prayer away.

'Just because we live in a so-called "Christian country", it doesn't mean that we are automatically Christians when we are born. It's nice if you can hang on to your faith when you are baptized as a child, but sadly, I think most people just use faith like an insurance policy, and only turn to God when they are in trouble. Personally, I just don't know how people survive life without a faith in God. I know I couldn't have. It's really not a case of trying to drum up some sort of blind belief within you, it's really all about discovering that we do have a purpose on this planet, and that someone else is in control. Once you come to see that, it's easy to have faith. Fortunately, God's love is not dependent on who or what we are.'

Bryan is a very humble and generous man, and is forever grateful for any small kindness shown to him. It is one of Derek Ware's strongest memories of Bryan's character. 'At a time when I was going through real financial difficulty due to a lack of work, he gave me five £5 notes and said a quiet "Thank you" for all the years I had supported him. I didn't expect to be repaid, but it's an indication of his belief in the value of friendship.'

'I've seen many of my friends die, but I have survived,' says Bryan, who is clearly grateful for the life that has been given him. He describes himself not as an optimist, but someone who always has hope. He is not an idealist who looks on the bright side of everything, but simply looks for the possible good in a given situation. Alongside writing his regular column in the *Weekly News*, in which he is given the freedom to comment on any current news item he chooses, he loves painting. His fear of being taken too seriously and criticized for something that is really only a hobby, prevents him from becoming too public about it. He was, however, awarded an Honorary Master of Arts degree by Bradford University in 1995 for contributions to the media.

'I have had a couple of exhibitions. People keep inviting me to show my work, but it's so terribly mediocre that I'm reluctant to do so. I'm not proud of them, but my work was shown at one exhibition between a Shephard and a Cunnio! They are two of the best painters we have, in my opinion. You can imagine my embarrassment, perhaps. I think if I wasn't Alf, no one would want to look at them. I paint using water-colour. I do the best I can and then I fiddle about with it. Charities often want them so that they can use them to raise money. I don't have a lot of technique, I just do it for fun really. I have been invited to submit work for a large exhibition soon, so I keep telling myself that I will have to pull my socks up and at least try to put something on paper. Norma does stunning work and we have many of her paintings around the house.

'What's discouraging is when I go round to exhibitions and see so many pictures of landscapes and flowers, and they all look the same. I don't want to paint those things, I want to do portraits, but I often think that I make a bit of a mess of it. My greatest ambition would be to paint a picture of our Lord, but I think I'll have to wait a bit before I'm able to do that!'

Ambition is something that Bryan views cautiously. 'I see ambitious people, and they just seem to destroy themselves. I suppose I could have done far better than I did, far faster if I was driven with ambition, but I just let people use me because I wanted to do the job they were offering. I had a lot of enthusiasm and energy, but this was often motivated by a concern for my family. It's important to have goals and to be assertive, but not at the cost of the rest of your life. My family have always been more important to me than any career.

'Fame is not worth a penny. I don't regret it, I'm just astonished by it. Fame can be a two-edged sword. Pretty meaningless really, particularly if it is not looked for. The whole business of fame has been a terrible burden for all the family, but it is a fact of life and we have tried to live with it. It's also very powerful, and I've seen it used to manipulate people. People in my position often get too big for themselves and pride takes over. I think all the difficulties I have faced throughout my life have kept my feet on the ground. I wake up each morning grateful for what I've been given. Ego is different though, and is important to an actor. Without ego an actor cannot survive. You must be persuaded that you are the best, or you've no chance. I love the professional respect of other people, it makes me give of my best.

'People often ask me if I need applause. The honest answer is that it is very gratifying when others tell me they enjoy my work. We all, I think, deserve applause from time to time, and I would certainly miss this affirmation. However, I really feel that actors, like painters, could work on a desert island, probably preparing for the day when the 'right moment pops up'! I'm used to being recognized almost everywhere I go now. Even on holiday in New Zealand once we were given the traditional Maori greeting. As we rubbed noses, members of the tribe said how much they enjoyed the series! However, if no one smiles or says hello, it automatically feels very strange and uncomfortable.

'In Rome once, nobody knew me, and it seemed so different from the way of life I was used to in Britain. On the Thursday a very Scottish voice asked me what I was doing in Rome, and it brought such a strange sense of reassurance. Although for some reason I have often been told that I do good work, curtain calls and uncalled-for adulation embarrass me, and I really do not need applause for its own sake. So it is a dichotomy of being given it and trying graciously to accept it.'

What Bryan does regret is that only some of his family share his faith. 'Some of our children seem to be drifting in their search for God's values and I am saddened by the fact that they don't have the strength of faith that Norma and I have enjoyed for so long. I tried to lead by example, but like everybody else, they have to make their own choice at the end of the day. They are a loving family, and we are all quite close. I could be despondent about their problem, but I am sustained and kept hopeful by my sometimes blind faith. This "blind" faith is not just accepting anything without reason or question, but accepting without being able to know all the answers or the outcome, and trusting that ultimately God knows what is best. My friend Bobby Ball says in his book *Christianity for Beginners** that "Faith in God is not automatic, it has to be something that you do, an act of the will … you don't have to leave your brain behind when you become a Christian … or start believing in impossible things."

'People often think that because I am famous I have a luxuriously problem-free life. Nothing could be further from the truth! Norma and I constantly battle through difficult issues, often struggling on against seemingly hopeless situations. We do feel the love of God, and are surrounded by the unwavering prayers of friends. At the end of the day all we can do is pray.'

It's obvious that prayer is everything to Bryan. 'Prayer is a life-line for me. Although we don't deserve it, we have been told to ask God for what we need. When it all boils down to it, and everything else is gone, prayer is actually the only thing we have left. My most common prayer apart from "Help!" is "Where do I go now?" I have seen him answer many "Help!"

* *Christianity for Beginners* by Tommy Cannon and Bobby Ball (Hodder & Stoughton, 1996).

prayers in my life, particularly at those times when work arrived at just the right time. Even more important is knowing that my life is in God's hands. So long as I am doing what God wants, I know I can't go far wrong. As the text on my dressing-room wall at *Coronation Street* reminds me, you can't rely on your own judgement, you have to wait for God to show you. When faced with difficult decisions, I like nothing better than to pray, telling God exactly what I would like, but then quietly asking "The Boss" what he thinks.'

In terms of his health problems, Bryan says that God is right here with him. 'I don't know what the future holds, but I do know who holds the future. Playing Alf gives me a sense of purpose, which is really to do what God desires. Even though I have been so unwell, and away from the studio for quite a while, the character of Alf is still there. He's still there as a person in people's lives. I am convinced that God has kept me in the business, and I feel very privileged because of this. Acting is one of the most difficult careers there is because of the emotional, physical and mental demands upon you. I would still do it all the same again, though. I only look at things on a daily basis these days, and I still worry a lot, but I try not to look too far into the future. Today has enough worries of its own. I try and live from day to day and moment to moment. It's important to me that Alf still brings so much enjoyment to others.'

Bryan sees his life not as something that will suddenly end, but more like the preparation for something that is beginning. 'Sometimes I think this life is almost like a dress rehearsal for heaven. There is so much to learn and understand. I think that maybe my job when I get up there will be to stand at the door taking the tickets!'

Ultimately, what gives Bryan his incredibly strong inner peace is the security of knowing that somebody bigger than

himself is in control. 'Even when you hope and pray that difficult things won't happen, you know that if they do, God will
give you the strength to get through them. I pray for my own
healing all the time, and for others too. I sometimes get
discouraged and maybe a little puzzled when I don't see my
prayers for healing answered, but I do realize that I can't tell
God what to do! I just have to hope, and wait until I get an
answer. There always is an answer, but it may not be the answer
I expect. Some answers to my prayers have been meeting the
right doctors at the right moment.

'I do lean back on my prayers in giving my situation up to
him. Sometimes I say, "I can't make it, God," but I must get
through for the sake of all those people supporting me. At
times I do feel like giving up. During this time I am learning,
like Job, to keep going. There is tremendous hope for the
future when I rely on God. I have never got angry at God for
letting my health problems arise, although I do question
things when a disaster like Dunblane happens. I haven't got an
answer, of course, and I think that if I was God I wouldn't have
allowed it to happen. But like the Bible says, "'My ways are not
your ways,' says the Lord." Some things are just too difficult
for us to understand. It's like the little boy offering to carry his
father's suitcase. His Dad smiles as he allows his son to try and
lift it up, knowing already that it is too much for him to carry.
After much huffing and puffing the little boy gives up,
conceding that it is too heavy for him to cope with, and his
Dad lifts it up by the handle as if it were a feather. Sometimes
we can't cope with carrying too much, and we just have to
leave it in our heavenly Father's hands.

'I don't find praying easy, of course. Lots of things stop me
from talking to God, but I know he's always interested in me.
I don't like long prayers and I think God must get so bored

with us prattling on sometimes. I like to say short prayers that just hand the situation over to him, and let him deal with it. He knows what's going on inside us and what our needs are anyway. For me prayer is like an everyday ongoing relationship with God. I chat to him all the time, rather than in a certain place in a certain direction at a certain time.'

Having said that, Bryan is often seen slipping into his local church in Manchester on the way back home from a day's recording. He enjoys popping into the quiet atmosphere of a church during the week for a quick pray, but the church they regularly attend is near their home in Shipley. 'It's the same church where G. K. Chesterton went. Norma and I try to get to church as regularly as we can, although this is often dictated by whether I have to work on the *Street* at weekends. I don't like working on a Sunday, but I don't really have a choice over this.'

Walking into church, he expects people to stare, and although he is used to it, he still finds it a bit uncomfortable when trying to worship privately. 'Our own church is much easier, as the people there are used to seeing "Alf" sitting there. They are also great at allowing me to be myself. I heard recently that a group from the church were going to ask for my help with something, and the Priest said, "No, this is Bryan's parish and we are not going to ask him to do anything. This is where he must be free to rest and feel at home, with no demands being made on him." I really appreciated that.

'When I can't get to church, I try and get together with other Christians for prayer. I still do this sometimes in my dressing-room at Granada, although I'm not there as often as I used to be. Praying together is important because our Lord has said that where two or three are gathered in his name, he will be with them. I like meeting with other Christians who are in the same business as well. It used to be a difficult profession in which to stand up and be counted as a Christian, but it's much more accepted these days, and there are many, many actors, comics, singers, writers and producers who hold a deep and sincere faith without putting their professionalism at risk. In fact, they are often respected for their faith rather than jeered at for it.'

Bryan explains that despite all the suffering around the world, he would say from his own personal experience that God is still a God of love, but that there is also an enemy of God who loves to destroy. His name is Satan, and he brings a lot of suffering into the world, alongside our own greed and mistakes. Bryan frowns and calls him 'Big Boots'.

'Big Boots is the enemy, the adversary who is always out to demolish any of the goodness left in our world. Even then, when terrible things happen, it's easy automatically to ascribe it to the devil, but often it's the result of mankind's own greed and selfishness. I do think the world is a poorer place because we have turned our backs on God. I think most people ignore God and his life-rules at their peril. Sometimes, with society in the state it's in, I think it's as bad as Sodom and Gomorrah. Again, I believe the answer is prayer. When we hand things over to God, we are giving him the chance to act, and this is when "Big Boots" really starts to tremble!

'Fortunately, so many difficulties can be turned round by God when we stop struggling and hand things over to him. When I did *Songs of Praise* for the BBC, I had just had one of the worst weeks of my life, as I was feeling so ill. I had not been able to sleep properly for over a week and could hardly move because of severe breathlessness. I was determined to do the programme, though, but I literally had to leave it all in the Lord's hands, as I was so poorly.

'It was suggested a couple of days beforehand that I should cancel out, but I decided that I would see it as an "act of faith" and go ahead if I possibly could. A car came and took Norma and me to the hotel that we were to stay in the night before the broadcast, but I couldn't get up the stairs and there was no lift. In the end they put me in one of those "dumb waiters" and changed my room over.

'Again I couldn't sleep, and I was really on edge that morning, and I told the programme makers that I didn't want to know what any of the questions were before the cameras started recording. I just wanted to let anything I said come directly from God. We all had a little prayer and put it in his hands. I knew it was important that I was honest in answering Pam Rhodes' questions and explained how frightened I had been during my illness, and how much I had depended on my faith.

'On the way home I saw a beautiful sunset, and it reminded me of the rainbow we saw on the way back from Lourdes, and of God's promise. When *Songs of Praise* went out there was an immense response from people who took heart from the fact that I was still there. Letters said they were sorry to see how ill I had been, but how much my recovery had been an inspiration to them and enabled them to put aside their own fears.

'One fear that I have not yet come to terms with is the shortness of time. When once things seemed interminable and endless, nowadays life passes in the twinkling of an eye. Part of that fear is the knowledge of how much irreplaceable time I waste. I appreciate every moment as precious these days. I am amazed that I am still here, and thank God for each new day that arrives.

'The most important thing to me at the moment is getting totally better and strong again, so that I can carry on enjoying life, and allowing Norma to enjoy life without the worry of all these problems surrounding my health. Norma's profound faith has been a great inspiration to me, and she has shown me that sometimes we need to stop trying, stop fighting, stop searching for the answers and just let go of the situation. For me as a Christian, it's even more important because when I let go, God can take over.'

Norma also discovered the importance of really letting go. 'After his first heart attack, I was absolutely adamant that he should give up the *Street* and retire. I felt he had given so much to the series, to charity, to the fans, and to everybody else, and that it was time for us now. I often got so tired of the problems associated with Bryan's celebrity status. I sometimes felt that our lives were not our own. It seemed that our private lives were always on public display. Then I understood how important work was for Bryan. I have my focus, my house, my garden, my family, my husband. Bryan's focus is his work. If I took that away from him, I could see that he would just shrivel up and give up. So long as the studio could allow him to take things a lot easier, I was happy for him to return, and it was encouraging that the studio really wanted him back.'

Well, return he did. On 9 June 1998 Bryan arrived at the gates of the Granada studios after an absence of nearly 14 months, and was received by an overwhelming number of embraces from the members of the cast. 'We really missed the old plonker,' said Curley Watts. 'It's really good to have Bryan back,' said Sue Nicholls (alias Alf's wife Audrey). 'It's a joy to have Bryan as my on-screen partner and I love Bryan's naughty sense of humour. He's had to cope with a horrid lot of hurdles recently, but he's come out the other side. It's been quite lonely playing just one half of a married couple, and there is a huge gap when he's not here. The *Street* was just not the same without him.'

I think most people agreed.

14

The Reverend Polewheel

Of audiences: 'They were really tough – they
used to tie their tomatoes on the end of a yo-yo,
so they could hit you twice.'
Bob Hope

Hope has been an essential ingredient in the life of Bryan
Mosley. So too has his love of schoolboy tomfoolery, which he
has never grown out of. The straight and worried face of Alf
hides an unchartered territory of mayhem and mirth, revealed
only to his most intimate associates.

Bryan's close friend Derek Ware, together with a dozen or so
other fight arrangers, had decided to form their own society
dedicated to the growing numbers of experts in the industry.
Derek had already created the stunt agency Havoc in 1965, but
the fighters and stunt men of the day were not properly repre-
sented, and it was clear that their interests were unique and
should be protected accordingly. In 1969 The Society of British
Fight Directors was formed with Bryan as a founder member. It
initially had no affiliation to other professional organizations
until the actors' union Equity gave it official recognition several
years later. It was later to become a strictly teaching body, but at
the time it held meetings to discuss various issues amongst its
growing membership. It also had a members' newsletter called

The Fight Director, which was to become the vehicle for some of Bryan's most outrageous pranks.

Hiding under the pseudonym of the Reverend Charles Polewheel, a supposedly amateur stunt arranger and producer, Bryan began to write beseeching letters to the editor of the newsletter, who happened to be Derek Ware. The first letter received from 'Polewheel' was printed in January 1978 and requested expert help for an amateur production of *Treasure Island*. It read:

> With luck we should be opening in early May and the setting will add to the production as it is in an inn yard. The only problem now is getting a stagecoach and four horses to back off the stage after they kill Blind Pew (incidentally, played by a man of 82). Billy Bones' spectacular fall down a flight of stairs promises to be very exciting, though naturally the actor will not try the fall until opening night...

Derek immediately smelled a rat, though many SBFD members where full of suggestions. This was followed by a second letter in the autumn of the same year:

> We have been compelled to postpone our production yet again as both Long John Silver and Blind Pew have developed ingrowing toenails and our Jim Hawkins' voice has broken. Our galleon should be ready within the next month or so and I am looking forward to seeing our Israel Hands fall from the rigging, which unfortunately will only be 28 feet or so. Readers may recall my problem with the coach and four, but we have decided, for safety's sake, to only hear the killing of Blind Pew. Billy Bones has retired from the enterprise on medical advice but we have now reinforced the stairs and I am confident they will not collapse again. I may have to take over

the part of Billy Bones but if so will only pretend to fall downstairs and will not actively engage in fencing.

'Polewheel' was next heard from in 1980 when he wrote:

Your good readers may recall my cries for help with our production of *Treasure Island*. The vicissitudes of our last production have welded our little band into some semblance of unity and now that all the legal expenses have been met after the collapse of the seating, I am glad to announce that our next production will be *Spartacus the Gladiator*. Our local zoo is kindly lending several animals and as they now have no less than three fully grown lions available, this should be quite interesting. My query is to enquire if anyone knows a reasonably safe way to set several Christians on fire? We would hope, of course, not to harm our members but it should look quite exciting as they would not be lit until late evening. My thanks for the anonymous gift of bandages from one of your readers, and for your information Blind Pew is now fully recovered and I'm glad to say his spine will soon be as good as new. The Squire's burns, which he sustained when the cannon ignited were, happily, superficial. The splendid fall performed by our Israel Hands on the first night was difficult to emulate by his understudy, but we all felt that the rope burns he sustained were worthily won. Meanwhile our original Israel is back on his feet and able to help in the post office. His face is no longer paralysed. One mistake we made was allowing our crew to partake so freely of the cider so kindly supplied by our good innkeeper. All suggestions for igniting the Christians will be gratefully received.

A year later *Spartacus the Gladiator* was still in rehearsal and the Reverend Polewheel poses the problem, 'What is the best way to sharpen machetes?' He goes on to tell how the burning of the Christians has been resolved:

> Our ingenious stage manager has fashioned several figures from rolled paper which are then covered with rags and saturated in paraffin (petrol is far too expensive now). That the effigies are successful has been proved, I venture, by the intervention of the nearby police who were utterly convinced that someone was actually cremating a body publicly. The gladiatorial armour is really fine but the blacksmith had an unfortunate accident when he attempted to swim the moat at the grange wearing a breastplate and helmet. However, antibiotics seem to be winning the day and I have no doubt that a full return to health will cheer him up. So we go on...

It was not until three years later that the bombshell came:

> Alas! Our production of *Spartacus the Gladiator* has been cancelled because of copyright matters and the lamentable lack of vestal maidens in the area. However, my intention is to present the opera *Aida*, with music provided by our Salvation Army quartet augmented by St Elsan's Junior Silver Ensemble. Our pyramid already towers above all but the parish steeple, but the local aerodrome have unfortunately complained to the authorities. However, one of our strongest supporters, the local Squire, holds some sway with the local council and assures me all will be well and feels that a short diversion over the estuary should not inconvenience the pilots too badly.

Six months later the *Aida* project has been abandoned in favour of a more modest enterprise, this time a medieval mystery play, *Noah's Flood*:

Miss Simpkins, the junior woodwork mistress at St Elsan's middle school, will use the spring term to fashion the ark … the Squire is already dredging the village pond preparatory to laying seating on the periphery, and our good innkeeper, Mr Stewer, seems happy to help in this enterprise. The ark will be a modest 27-foot-long model and our constable will be responsible for the wickerwork embellishments sketched by Miss Simpkins. We are all excited, as this year there will be no physical combat, so what can go wrong?

Apparently *Noah's Flood* was a success, or at least singularly free from mishap, as Derek did not hear from the Reverend Polewheel again for some time. Instead there flowed an interestingly strange series of letters from those requesting membership of the Society of British Fight Directors. Each letter had curiously different handwriting, yet members of the Society were very suspicious that the source was the same. The first manuscript had the Salvation Army base in London as its host address:

Dear Mr Ware

I understand that you will soon be opening an agency for stuntmen, and, although I have never really done anything since I lost my leg fighting a hippo (*Adventures of Buddy*, 1922), I wonder if you might be able to use me. Incidentally, I lost my hand in the Zulu sequences in *Further Adventures of Buddy* (1946), but that was an accident.

My last fall was from the roof of the Palace Attercliffe when I was working on the demolishment of the premises (1951). (I lost my left eye there, but only a small scar is left. The glass one nearly matches my other eye too.) I am still a good swimmer and nearly got work on the recent James Bond film *Thunder Guts*, but they were wanting people with ears. (Lost one (R) fighting a gorilla in *The Last of Buddy*, 1947.)

However, as you can imagine, I am not very good at diving, as the crutch always fouls things up. I also used to be a first-class pistol shot until I lost my finger (trigger) in a phone box (I couldn't get the money either).

I am 4 ft. 11¾ in. tall, but, with lifts, can manage 6 ft. 3¼ in. tall. I have my own wig (lost my hair in the fire sequence of *Gone With the Wind* – send-up of the MGM film of the same name, never distributed) and quite extensive wardrobe (i.e. topper and opera cloak worn by Claude Raines in *Phantom of the Opera*, fangs worn by Bela Lugosi in *Dracula*, etc., etc.). I enclose a recent photo (made up to look younger). I am not on the telephone at present, but anyone will tell you where to find me.

Yours sincerely

Dexter Burk.

One is amazed at the fact that Derek Ware, having known Bryan's dangerous sense of humour, would even have considered using Bryan for a job reference, but this he did. Bryan happily agreed and offered to send his friend a copy of the letter he had passed on directly to Derek's prospective employers. Imagine Derek's astonishment when he received the scrawled note (in pencil on a badly stained piece of white paper) and read the following:

To whom it may concern

My mate Derek Ware is applying for the job of Artistic Director. Though I have never seen any of his paintings I am sure he can hold the job down, as he helps his lady wife when she decorates. Before he started drinking he nearly always got to the Theatre before the half, and he is a smashing bloke to have around while the tea is being brewed. He is very quick at inventing dialogue, and this has saved him many times. He is

also very generous when he has had a few. He once lent me
ten bob, before he fell on hard times. He is a very comical
actor and I have seen him get laughs in every part he ever
played, including *Oedipus Rex* and *Tamboline*. He also tap
dances.

Please give him a break as he is really getting on my nerves.
Obliged,

B. Windrush

Suddenly the Reverend Charles Polewheel pops up again after
an absence of three years. It was 1986, and this time he was in
something of a quandary as to the choice of subject for the
next production:

We are resolved to be more prudent and modest than in the
past and have considered staging *Moby Dick* or *Nanook Of The
North*. We have at last reached a more or less unanimous decision to essay a drama to be written by Miss Loosens, our
Primary Headmistress, to be entitled *To The Mountains With
The Mounties*. This will be set in the foothills of Alaska and
will incorporate all the elements of *Nanook* besides encounters with Red Indians, Eskimos and 'low life' from Nova
Scotia. The Squire has offered to secure a replica of a whale.
His determination to play Captain Ahab will not be discouraged, so we hope he will be towed around the bay during the
snowstorm that we hope to produce when our hero, Lomond
of the Mounties, is crossing Niagara Falls to rescue an old lady
at risk in a barrel. We would be grateful for any suggestions
readers might have to offer, as we hope to show a collision
between two railway engines and a cattle stampede. Our space
is somewhat limited, but where there's a will there's a way...

Evidently, the logistics of staging the above could not be overcome, even with Polewheel's unbounded optimism, as the
next offering is to be *Carmen*:

> Already the Squire has arranged (from his bed in the cottage
> hospital for some reason) for the fattening up of several of his
> bulls in the hope that he will have a convincingly savage crea-
> ture for our plucky constable to fight each evening. Can any of
> your readers suggest a way to make a competent *veronica* or
> *pas a doubles*? The terms, I am aware, are incorrect but we
> would be glad to hear from any budding aficionado. Indeed,
> we would happily welcome anyone troubling to join us and
> demonstrate the necessary passes. Our bull ring is almost
> completed and our audience will sit around it whilst cigarette
> girls and muleteers walk among them. Miss Hepple is teaching
> her class the best method of rolling cigarettes and our Carmen,
> Miss Diddle, has joined a nearby Weight Watchers to shed a
> few stones for the first night. We plan to have no less than 30
> toreadors. So, Excelsior! We hope to hear from you. Thank
> you again for the Radian B and the kneepad…

In the autumn of the same year came the sad but not unexpected news:

> Alas! *Carmen* has been cancelled, due to the intervention of
> the RSPCA. Originally, after the bull had been slaughtered
> humanely, we thought of employing a skin with two burly
> fellows to, as it were, ape the bull. However, our doughty
> Squire decided that this would lessen the impact of his idea of
> employing several bulls and possibly inviting a visiting
> matador to appear in the production. We have looked at
> several alternative ideas including *Torquemada and the*
> *Spanish Inquisition* (Miss Purler thought that the human

rights people might object). We are now considering *Cortez*, to be written by our local librarian, Miss Wortle. This will have the advantage of being set in dense jungle. Our Squire has suggested a display of poisonous serpents and spiders and has already, in his enthusiasm, procured an iguana which he keeps in his conservatory, much to the dismay of his three Doberman. Any suggestions as to armour and accoutrement will be welcomed. Mrs Levington has already begun drawing costumes, though I personally feel that mere beads will not be enough for our convent girls as the evenings draw in and the gnats abound. Well, we shall see. Certainly the costume fittings may prove interesting. As summer begins our local fields are filled with limpists and dogpugh, the trees are in blossom and even the new abattoir has a certain gaiety. We have much to be thankful for in our tiny hamlet. All are welcome.

Charles Polewheel (Revd)

PS. Many thanks to your kind reader for sending us the wheelchair, which may prove useful if we ever require a chariot. The Squire already has three or four of his own, so perhaps we could consider revising *Ben Hur*. We shall see.

This was to be the last of the Reverend Polewheel as, unfortunately, *The Fight Director* ceased publication shortly afterwards. However, there was one final letter that was found buried under a pile of old photographs owned by Bryan. It was never forwarded on to the Society, maybe because it was the most risqué of all:

Gentleman, alas! The local authority has banned our intended production, *Bang – the story of Krakatana*. Our indomitable squire will recover in time after the dreadful explosions, but the Manor House is, sadly, gutted. Miss Muffler is organizing tea mornings and good-as-new parties to help pay for some of the damage. However, the litigation promises to prove expensive, as the local farmers are quite incensed by the loss of livestock and damaged outbuildings. As Lady Whiffen remarked, they seem to be over-reacting. All the explosives have been confiscated and the vendors, unhappily, are already incarcerated hither and thither. The Colonel has, I understand, gone to live in San Salvador. 'Ah well,' as Miss Carter quipped with some levity, 'on to the next orgy!'

This brings me to my next intended production, *The Rape of the Vestals*. We require a number of nubile but reasonably chaste maidens for this epic. Unfortunately the headmistress at St Vulpine's is resisting my blandishments to involve her sixth-formers again. The silly girls who were expelled after our ill-fated *Lysistrata* are not available as they are still on probation, though I understand that two or three are living in Buenos Aires.

Well, our stage is open. The couches await and we have no shortage of youths available to play the lusty soldiery. Perhaps some of your readers could persuade wives or sweethearts to join us. There are many here who would rejoice.

Cordial Best Wishes.

In addition to the huge enjoyment derived from the ludicrous situations, Bryan, in 10 years, and with the minimum amount of description, was able to build up a microcosm of a mythical village, complete with a population of not-so-exaggerated characters. The saturnine but faithful Squire; the Constable, so willing that he lost his job and was subsequently referred to as 'our ex-Constable'; Miss Simpkins, Miss Loosens, Mrs Levington, Miss Hepple and Miss Biddle, all devoted to the eternally optimistic Reverend Charles Polewheel.

15

The End of an Era

By perseverance the snail reached the ark.
Charles Spurgeon

What has encouraged me more than anything else in unwrapping the secrets of Bryan's life is his perseverance. The looks on the faces of the *Coronation Street* cast and crew on his first day back after his long illness said it all. The fact that he had arrived back at work suffering from a stomach bug after a holiday trip to Ireland just shows the determination of the man to get on with the job and get on with life.

It is his perseverance that saw him through the pressure of going against the popular tide of expected career prospects. It was a relentless determination that got him through the battles of proving to his in-laws that he was a good provider for his wife and family. It was his persistence that saw him make his mark first in the theatre world, then in films and eventually in television. Finally it was his steadfast sense of hope that got him through one of the most critical periods of his life, when faced with the possibility of death.

And yet what is most astonishing is not Bryan's determination to push through all obstacles, as so many in his profession have done, but the fact that he successfully combines this with a sense of humility and trust. He will not abuse others in his quest for the goal; rather he will stand back and let others take the stage. True, he is beset with the performer's curse of having a low opinion of himself, but this often has the effect in others of causing them to ill-treat those around them. Not so Bryan. His concern and compassion for those with whom he comes into daily contact is the practical out-working of his faith in a God whom he knows loves him deeply. I would like to take a page out of Bryan's book of life, to learn to have the perfect mix of perseverance with humility, and to understand that the past is not meant to be a hammock, but a springboard.

Indeed, it was this view of life that was to sustain him as he agonized over making one of the biggest decisions of his life and career. By the summer of 1998 studio bosses at Granada Television were becoming increasingly concerned about Bryan's fragile health and the stress that he would be put under by a proper working regime back on the programme. Viewers themselves were shocked at how ill Alf looked on screen when he arrived back after his health break. Having lost nearly five stone, and looking quite pale, it was obvious that he had not fully recovered, and many feared that his illness was terminal.

It was agreed that Bryan would be used on a reduced basis, appearing in a few episodes at a time. In reality this meant that Bryan would on average spend a few days in the studio or on location, followed by a few weeks off. Granada was well in tune with the fact that Alf was one of their best characters, greatly loved by *Street* fans the world over, and were loath to write him out of the programme.

Monitoring the situation over the next few months, studio producers had regular meetings with Bryan. Medical experts were brought in to assess his condition alongside his own doctor, and a studio nurse at Granada would keep a beady eye on Bryan whenever he was working there. The most obvious sign of Bryan's illness, apart from his looks (which were improved on screen by the extra application of make-up), was the slowness with which he walked and his extreme bouts of breathlessness. This was an extremely worrying symptom for other members of the cast, and subsequently tension in the studio rose when Bryan was recording his scenes. Because of their concern for him, the other cast members found it difficult to focus on their own performances. There was no animosity, however, as the cast all loved him dearly. They would have been shocked to see him removed from the show, and only wanted him to make a speedy recovery.

Over the next few weeks Bryan's health began to improve, and by the time a ten-week stint of holiday was about to commence in late August, he was looking better than ever. His body had stabilized to the point where he could live a reasonably normal life, and his old comic banter when speaking with friends had returned.

Despite this recovery, Bryan began to face the fact that the pace that had been required of him in the past was now out of reach. The pressure of being a huge soap star, with all its attachments and responsibilities, the weight of learning new lines, scenes and situations, and the energy required in simply performing on a regular basis, could well prove too much for him to cope with. An actor never really retires anyway, he told himself. Like a horse, a performer has to be shot to be stopped. If he were to stop appearances on the *Street*, there may well be other one-off appearances that he would be asked to do, and could possibly consider.

Yet the *Street* had been his total focus for so long, and he continued to reflect on all that it meant to him. He was very proud of being part of a television legend, and he had grown to love those he had worked with. He considered that the entire cast had been exceptional actors, with one or two achieving 'greatness', he thought. Familiar faces filled his thoughts as his mind thumbed through a short cast-list of favourites.

'Eileen Derbyshire and her husband Tom are great friends. Betty Driver is the one who, it seems, never puts a foot wrong. Bill Roach is my giggling pal. Roy Barraclough also makes me laugh to tears. Bill Tarney, Liz Dawn and Helen Worth have been towers of strength to me. Kevin Kennedy kept us all cheerful with his wise-cracks. And Shaun Wilson is a superb, unassuming actor with a great talent for painting.'

Sue Nicholls was conscious more than most of Bryan's health struggles. Playing his screen wife for so many years, she was always aware of the big question mark that continually loomed over Bryan's future, like a black cloud waiting to burst. She missed Bryan's company and fondly remembered the little idiosyncrasies that made him such fun to work with. The fact that they knew each other so well actually meant that their scenes together were the easiest ones to perform. 'I always knew instinctively how Bryan would do something,' Sue recalls. 'At the start of the week, when I received my script, I could see how many scenes Bryan and I had, and judge whether it would be an easy week or not. Our performances as man and wife always fitted so well, but we both wish the characters of Alf and Audrey had been developed more as a couple.'

Sue was also well aware of the fact that Bryan's future on the *Street* had to be decided one way or the other, and secretly wondered how long Bryan could continue in bad health. Bryan himself was conscious of the problems that his health created for the cast, wondered what they might be saying behind his back, and was concerned that at times his disability may have stretched their patience. Sue, he reflected, 'had the patience of a saint during my illness, and I am so grateful to her for that.'

Though the opportunities to go out together socially were few, the cast had remained very close and protective of one another. As other names, faces and frozen moments of time snapped into place in Bryan's memories, he knew without a doubt that he would miss them all if he were to leave. He had on several occasions said to the press that because the *Street* was in his blood, he would never stop. 'It gives me something to get up for,' he said. 'I'd become a vegetable if I quit.' Yet by early October 1998 this was precisely what he was considering.

His illness had also afforded him time to take an objective look at television today. As he watched the 'box' in his front room, neatly encased in a cabinet with teak doors, to hide the screen away when he really wanted to 'switch off', he was surprised at how much had changed over 37 years. It seemed to him that the golden age of hope and excitement had passed by. Standards had slipped both morally and artistically, and he felt that some of the programmes being produced were disgraceful and could lead society into an accelerating spiral of decadence. Was it true, Bryan pondered, that accountants were now running television?

Films too, had lost the magic they once held in Bryan's eyes. He considered that good story-lines and creative characters are often replaced by special effects and frenetic editing. Would they all come to their senses one day and again give reassurance and good example to the world we all inhabit? He really hoped so.

Now, having met with studio bosses once more, he was in agreement that it was perhaps time that Alf considered hanging up his trilby. Also in agreement were his family, and particularly Norma, who had for some time tried to convince Bryan that he should call it a day and start to enjoy a proper retirement. After all, thought Bryan, 67 is a very respectable age to bow out. Recent family difficulties had also put Bryan and Norma under extra demand, and it was felt that Bryan's release from the *Street* would be a great relief. Their children, Jacqueline, Simone, Helen, David, Bernard and Leonard, had all gone on to different careers, several related to the performing arts or teaching, as one might expect. Grand-children Alexander, Benjamin, Charlotte, Roseanna, Tom and Lauren created the mixture of pride, worry and joy that all grandparents experience. Being free from the *Street* would also give Bryan more time to be with the family he loved so dearly.

It was still no easy decision for Bryan, however, and as he weighed up all the pros and cons, once more he turned to his Maker for help and reassurance. It was God, he felt, who had opened the door for Alf, and it was God who would close it, he decided. One October morning, whilst Norma was out shop-ping, he sat alone in the favourite chair of his Shipley home and quietly prayed. In the silence, broken only by a few bursts of song from a nearby bird, his thoughts drifted over 37 years of a character that had become a part of himself. He knew that there would be a deep sense of sadness and loss were he to stop playing Alf. If he pulled out of the series there was bound to be a period of grief and even an atmosphere of bereavement for a while. Would he be able to cope with the emptiness? Alongside this was the fear that he may suddenly be taken ill again and be robbed of choosing how the character should be phased out. As a shaft of sunlight pushed through the autumnal trees and into his front room, Bryan knew in his heart what he should do. When Norma returned from her trip he told her the good news, and they embraced as a symbol of solidarity and affection.

Two days later Bryan met the Granada bosses once more. There was a mixture of relief and sadness as Bryan gave them his decision. All that was left to agree on now was how Alf should be written out of the series. Bryan was pleased to be involved in this process, and after some discussion, he was instrumental in the conclusion that his beloved character should pass away peacefully. It was important to Bryan, and he felt to his fans, that for Alf, who held such standing and esteem on the *Street*, an untimely or violent death was not appropriate. He should leave with the dignity and respect that he deserved.

Discussions over someone else's death are an amazing oddity, rarely encountered by anyone outside the world of script-writers, novelists and criminals. Strangely, Bryan was not at all disturbed to be a party in these deliberations, rather seeing his involvement in them as an honour that very few actors ever enjoy. Deciding on 'his own' death was to give Bryan the extra energy, motivation and excitement that he needed to execute the task to the best of his ability.

He had twice before played characters who had died on screen. One famous incident concerned the popular sixties' police series *Z-Cars*. The episode in question was considered to be so violent for its early evening transmission slot on BBC 1 that it raised a historic discussion in the House of Commons after being screened. In 'Affray' Bryan, playing a hated criminal, had driven a 20-ton low-loader into a brick wall and was slowly dying on camera as the police arrived. Together with stunt driver Stan Hollingsworth, they managed to demolish an entire 10-foot garden wall in one camera shot. What makes Bryan chuckle when reminiscing over this episode is the fact that the make-up girl had no 'blood' in her kit. 'When we came to do the scene, she apologized for her mistake and smeared bright red lipstick over my face instead! I must be the only actor who has "died" on television with a trickle of lipstick pouring out of his wounds!'

With the news of his departure from the *Street* imminently becoming public, Bryan telephoned his screen wife Audrey to break the news. 'I was shocked and saddened at first,' Sue says. 'I realized that although he would be yearned for by the fans, it would be me who would miss him the most. I will always treasure memories of working with Bryan and will have him to thank that my own character has been around for so long. It was very difficult to think of letting him go, yet Alf had to go for the sake of Bryan's health.'

Indeed, the whole cast were saddened by the news, but like all other *Coronation Street* story-lines, it was agreed that the story of Alf's demise should be kept well 'under wraps'. The element of surprise should be kept as long as possible, though in reality those around the table knew that such a big story could not be kept hidden for long. But if the news of Alf's imminent death became public, at least the exact events leading up to it could surely be concealed.

At home in Shipley three days later it was Bryan who suddenly experienced the power that such knowledge contained. Two newspaper reporters knocked at his front door, and immediately took photographs of the bemused Bryan as he answered. As they fired questions at the confused actor to force out the truth of Alf's departure, Bryan could only stutter, 'It's all news to me!' As Bryan pushed the front door shut, he was angered and then saddened by the fact that the story had been leaked so soon.

The following day, Tuesday 13 October, the *Mirror* reported on its front page the news, '*Street* to kill off Alf in TV shock'. The paper also contained a two-page spread of Alf over the years, with accompanying comments on how much he would be missed. They reported that Alf would die peacefully in his armchair on New Year's Eve 1998, and predicted that the nation would be in mourning.

The result of this news was that Bryan's home was immediately transformed from being a place of rest and tranquillity into bedlam. With his front garden besieged by reporters and photographers from every newspaper imaginable, his telephone rang constantly with shocked friends and cast members wanting to confirm that there was truth in the story.

It was true. Alf was finally going to be laid to rest, and Bryan was actually starting to look forward to the drama of it all. Whilst there was always the possibility that Granada would change the way Alf retired from the screen, just to confound the press, the script finally arrived on Bryan's doorstep. It couldn't have arrived soon enough, as Bryan was anxious to familiarize himself with the text and get on with the job. Two weeks later Bryan was in the studio with an atmosphere of excitement and expectancy amongst the cast. That day, 4 December, brought to the surface a hidden and very deep sadness at the thought of Alf's demise. Knowing smiles followed Bryan's every move, as the red-carpet treatment was laid on by everyone present.

The final moments of Alf's life were recorded in one solemn 'take'. As he slumped in the old armchair at his granddaughter's home, the New Year celebrations slowly came to a halt when it was realized that Alf had quietly slipped away. As the closing credits would start to roll, cast, crew, cameramen, producers and writers continued to stare at the still figure of Bryan, and the tense atmosphere in the studio could be felt in the frozen silence. Suddenly, to everyone's surprise, Bryan sat up and shouted a loud 'Boo!' The nervous jerks of shock were quickly replaced by uncontrolled laughter, and the atmosphere was transformed from deadly mourning to frivolous fun. Bryan, always the practical joker, used every opportunity to the very end.

A glamorous after-studio surprise party was held in Bryan's honour that night. Surrounded by those with whom he had worked for so many happy years, David Hanson, the *Coronation Street* producer, presented Bryan with the biggest bunch of white lilies ever seen. The cast had organized a cake to be made in the shape of Alf's trilby, and Shaun Wilson had made a book of photographs of the entire cast, all wearing Alf's hat. For Bryan it was a 'once in a lifetime' occasion. 'I'll never forget my final bow as Alfie,' he says fondly.

Alf's final episode was watched by nearly 19 million viewers. Bryan revelled in all the fuss, and in its own way the storm that had been provoked was just confirmation that 'Alf', and in particular Bryan's own contribution to British television history, was certain to be remembered for a very long time.

Bryan's personal prayer

Lord Jesus, I come before you, just as I am.
I am sorry for all I have done wrong, please forgive me.
In your name, and with your help, I forgive
all others for what they have done against me.
Come Lord Jesus, and fill me anew with your Holy Spirit.
Amen.

Afterword

Bryan told me that one day he would be on *News at Ten*. His words came true on 9 February 1999 when the sad news of his death was announced by anchorman Trevor McDonald. The nation mourned, and tributes from *Coronation Street* co-stars flooded in. 'He was a great man and a great pal. He always made us laugh,' commented Kevin Kennedy, the show's Curley Watts. Bill Roach, alias Ken Barlow, was deeply saddened. 'He was a great actor, and he will be sorely missed,' he said. Bryan's professionalism, his determination and his faith had won him real friendships in and out of the business world-wide.

Bryan and Norma had been on their way to their bank in order to draw holiday money for one of their beloved holiday trips abroad. This time it was to Venice, Bryan had told me the day before, a city they both especially loved because of its romantic attachments. Bryan and Norma were great romantics, and Bryan would take up every opportunity to display the deep love he had for his wife. The last time I accompanied him to one of his regular hospital check-ups he stopped at the hospital's retail area to browse over books on television and comedy, and then made his way directly to the florist. The woman who served him knew who he was, not just because he was a famous face, but because he had obviously been a regular visitor. He had bought flowers for Norma here on many occasions, and the shop assistant even enquired after the welfare of his wife. With a big grin, Bryan said Norma was looking as lovely as ever, and would appreciate the wonderful lilies that had been so carefully wrapped.

On the way back to the car, the lilies were nearly blown away in the sudden gusts of wind that were a sign of winter. Strangely, these hospital visits were a source of real comfort to Bryan, who felt that he was well on the road to recovery. Each blood test, each echo-cardiogram, showed signs of improvement that encouraged Bryan to think positively of the future. He always kept his feet on the ground, however, and was aware that, despite the fact that his days were certainly limited, it was 'up to him upstairs to say when I go'. Until then, Bryan decided, he would not consider what was 'around the corner' – he would live life to the full.

The tabloid newspaper assumptions that Bryan's death was caused by his retirement from *Coronation Street* were wrong. He was certainly sad to leave the show, but once he had accepted that it was in his best interests to do so, he settled into a new world of hope and happiness. He was so pleased about the prospect of spending more time with Norma, and they had a whole host of trips planned, from amazing train journeys to pilgrimages rediscovering favourite haunts. I had mentioned to him that just because Alf's career had come to an end, it didn't mean Bryan's had too. He agreed and set about discussing with his agent new possibilities for work, ambitions unfulfilled, and the opportunity of a television advert. There was much still to do.

Bryan was also incredibly excited about this book, and had played such a big part in it from the moment it was proposed. He was very proud of *Street Life*, not in a haughty way, but in what he was able to achieve in his life. He wanted to show that you can do almost anything if you put your mind to it. He was anxious that readers should be able to discover the real Bryan and not 'Alf'. He also wanted his readers to know that he had always acknowledged the central role God had played in his life, and that this was why he was especially blessed. He had talent, yes, but it was 'God who opened the doors'.

The launch date for *Street Life* had been set, and he was like a child looking forward to a birthday, telephoning me every few days to check that there was nothing else he should be doing to help the process. We had our final discussion the day before he died. I reassured him that it was all in order, that it was now out of our hands. We just had to await the launch party, on the set of *Coronation Street* in Manchester. He was happy to let it go. I suggested we had a quiet, secret meal together to celebrate, and he asked if I could stay for a few days in Shipley. Bryan liked a party.

My deepest personal sadness is that he didn't get to see this book published – but what better tribute could there be to a man who loved so much and was so loved himself? Through all his difficulties and pain he was able to let God's light shine through and warm those around him. He lived in public and he died in public, but I am confident that he is now enjoying the delights of a heavenly party the likes of which he has never seen before. God bless you, Bryan.

Chris Gidney
11 February 1999

BRIAN MOSLEY:
Filmography and Factfile

Bryan's career has spanned more than 40 years. He has appeared in more than 100 theatre plays, 20 films and literally hundreds of television dramas and comedies, including an established part in the longest-running television series in history, and appeared as Alf more than 3,000 times. *Coronation Street* was a very big part of his life, but this is not to forget all the other appearances which made him the man he was. The following list of facts, films and fun was compiled by a whole host of friends and fans.

Bryan's theatre career

The Byre Theatre (1950–51)
Squaring the Circle; *The Heart of Midlothian*; *Macbeth*; *The Importance of Being Earnest*; *Mary Rose*; *The Masque of St Andrews*.

Bradford Children's Theatre School Tour
The Little Dragon; *Twelfth Night*; *Seraphino*; *The Tenth Province*; *The Golden Goose*; *Lilliom*.

Perth Repertory Company (1955–6)
Seagulls over Sorrento; *On the Spot*; *To Live in Peace*; *Reluctant Heroes*; *The Wooden Dish*; *Othello*; *Castle in the Air*; *Cinderella*; *Two Dozen Red Roses*.

Harry Hanson's Repertory Company (1956)
Ask Your Dad; Rebecca.

York Repertory Company (various years)
The Teahouse of August Moon; Aladdin; Macbeth; Henry IV Parts 1 & 2; The Man Who Came To Dinner; Henry V; Twelfth Night; The French Mistress; Worm's Eye View; Hot and Cold in all Rooms; Black Comedy; The Rainmaker; Ruffian on the Stairs; Romeo & Juliet.

Scarborough Repertory Company
Spring & Port Wine; Bed, Board & Romance; Charlie's Aunt.

Derby Repertory Company
La Malade Imajinaire.

White Rose Theatre, Harrogate
Dusty Ermine; Arsenic & Old Lace.

Butlins, Clacton
Cosh Boy; The Late Edwina Black; Sailor Beware; While The Sun Shines.

Bryan's films

Directed by John Schlessinger: *A Kind of Loving; Billy Liar; Far From The Madding Crowd.*
Directed by Mike Hodges: *Get Carter.*
Directed by Lindsay Anderson: *This Sporting Life.*
Directed by Christopher Miles: *Up Jumped A Swagman.*
Directed by Joe McGrath: *30 is a Dangerous Age, Cynthia; The Bliss of Mrs Blossom.*
Directed by Betty Box: *Rattle of a Simple Man.*
Directed by Peter Watkins: *Privilege.*

Also: *Diamonds Are For Breakfast.*
Where The Bullets Fly.

Bryan's television appearances

Coronation Street (more than 3,000 episodes); *Crossroads*;
The Plane Makers; *Shadow Squad*; *The Men From Room 13*;
Hadleigh; *Adam Adamant*; *The Saint*; *The Avengers*;
Armchair Theatre (several episodes); *Play of the Week* (several
episodes); *The Rise & Fall of Nellie Brown*; *The High Game*;
Romeo & Juliet; *The Villains*; *Z-Cars* (several episodes); *Dr
Who* (several episodes); *Treasure Island*; *The Spread of the
Eagle*; *The Arthur Haynes Show*; *It's A Square World*; *The
Harry Worth Show*; *The Jimmy Clitheroe Show*; *The Dick
Emery Show*; *The Peter Butterworth Show*; *The Worker*; *No
Hiding Place*; *Songs of Praise*; *This is Your Life* (including his
own!); *The VIPs*; *The Gloria Hunniford Show.*

… And literally thousands of personal appearances on stage,
screen and radio since 1951.

Alf's history

Much to Bryan's amusement and delight, the character of Alf
was taken very seriously by 'Corrie' buffs around the world.
There are even some interesting parallels with Bryan's own
personal life-journey, as revealed here.

July 1979: After the lorry crash, Alf decides to leave the
GPO. As he was an Assistant Inspector, he was entitled to a fair
amount of money. If he took early retirement he would get
£1,800 p.a. and £5,000 at the age of 60 – but he was hoping to

be retired on medical grounds, when he would get £2,000 p.a. and a £6,000 lump sum immediately.

Alf used to run the corner shop in *Coronation Street* with his second wife, Renee. It was the place where he was happiest. He'd be there all hours, but the shop wasn't good enough for Audrey, and she persuaded him to sell it. This didn't last long, though. He bought it back again when Brendan Scott (former Bettabuy employee) got over-stressed and had a heart attack. Audrey finally made him sell it again, this time to Reg Holdsworth, another Bettabuy employee who was made redundant.

Alf was also a councillor, and elected Mayor of Weatherfield. As a shopkeeper, Alf was a member of WARTS (Weatherfield Association of Retail Traders). So there were always lots of functions for him to go to, and he did enjoy them, as he liked a good feed. Audrey kept putting him on diets, but they didn't last very long.

Audrey wasn't so keen on the mayoral functions, finding them boring. She did, however, love being Lady Mayoress (well, she got to buy lots of hats) and was mortified when Alf sacked her for not performing her duties properly and got Betty Turpin in instead.

The highlight of Alf's career was when he was awarded the OBE and went to the Palace to receive it. Now he's got a street named after him, Alfred Roberts Wynde.

Alf died quietly and peacefully on 31 December 1998. He would have been sad to have missed seeing the Millennium dawn, but perhaps all the fuss would have proved too much of an irritation and worry for him.

Character anniversaries

8 October 1926: Alfred Sydney Roberts is born.

18 September 1972: Phyliss Roberts, Alf's first wife, dies of cancer.

20 March 1978: Alf Roberts marries Renee Bradshaw, owner of the Corner Shop.

30 July 1980: Renee Bradshaw dies.

23 December 1985: Audrey Potter marries Alf Sydney Roberts. Gail Tilsley was her witness.

31 December 1998: Alf Sydney Roberts dies peacefully, aged 72.

A potted history of the *Street*

It's one of the world's most famous and long-running television programmes. *Coronation Street*, or the *Street*, as it is affectionately known by its millions of fans, has been running continuously since 9 December 1960.

The reason for its longevity is probably that the characters are believable and down to earth. They are the type of people you would meet on your own street or have come into contact with in your life. This is not found in most North American soap operas, where half of the cast are millionaires and all have been in jail for murdering someone.

Coronation Street has a huge following throughout the world, particularly in those countries that have a large 'ex-pat' population. Canada, Australia, New Zealand and the United States have a large number of fans. It won the BAFTA Award for Best Television Soap again in October 1998.

The birth of the *Street*

Coronation Street was the brainchild of Tony Warren, a former child actor who in 1958 began working for Granada Television in Manchester. Warren was doing some writing, and a casting director made arrangements for him to meet with Harry Elton, a Canadian producer whose job was to find talent. Elton listened to Warren and, by Warren's own admission, *Coronation Street* would 'never have seen the light of day' had it not been for Elton.

Warren wrote some detective/police shows and also some 'Biggles' adventures. Granada was in the midst of an experiment and offered Warren a one-year exclusive contract which provided him with security, and in return Granada received exclusive rights to everything he wrote. This is how Granada acquired *Coronation Street*. Warren's response to his loss of these rights was, 'I would have been very bad at being a millionaire.'

Warren named the show *Florizel Street* when getting it prepared for Granada. The scripts and ideas were prepared in secrecy, and finally four episodes were written to present to Granada.

Elton then went to the Granada executives with the concept and with a one-paragraph synopsis of the series. The paragraph read: 'A fascinating freemasonry, a volume of unwritten rules. These are the driving forces behind the life in a working-class street in the North of England. The purpose of *Florizel Street* is to examine a community of this nature, and to entertain.'

Granada, which had the licence to transmit to most of Northern England, had made a commitment to reflect life in the North and to bring employment to the area. The programming was not very representative of the North and most of the actors were from the South. Warren and Elton saw the local actors, of whom there were many, as a great source of talent for the series.

It was decided that two pilot episodes would be aired, and if they were successful, another 12 could be written. A production team was put together, and Stuart Latham became producer. Harry Kershaw, a writer from the North, worked with Warren. Dennis Parkin and Kershaw toured the Salford area along with Warren, looking for a street that would match the vision they had for the series. They settled on Archie Street in the Ordsall district. It was used for the opening shots of the series, and the very few exterior shots.

There was concern as the first episode's airing came close, and television sets were placed around Granada and staff were asked to watch and critique the show. The show was greeted favourably by a factor of 10:1, and the show was on again...

On Friday 9 December 1960 at 7 p.m. the familiar *Coronation Street* theme was heard for the first time. Thirty-five years later it is still going strong and is watched all over the world, having become the longest-running TV show in the UK. It has recently celebrated 35 years as the top soap, with an average of 20 million viewers per episode. It is filmed at Granada Studios, Manchester. Episode 4,000 was shown on Monday 15 April 1996.

Alf Sydney Roberts

- Played by Bryan Mosley.
- Appeared: February 1961 onwards.
- Born: 1926.
- Twice Mayor of Weatherfield.
- Marriages: 1. Phyllis. 2. Renee Bradshaw. 3. Audrey Potter (1985).

- Started off as a GPO sorter. Renee's death gave him the corner shop.
- President (1990) and member of WARTS. When he first met Denise Osbourne he asked her: 'Have you considered WARTS?'
- When he sold his shop he wanted to preserve his store sign for posterity.
- The character was once described as the kind of fellow who could teach at Sunday school.

The Weatherfield Town Council wanted to give Alf a lasting name in the town in recognition of his long service. The Council proposed changing the name of Mayfair to Alf Roberts' Place, but the proposal was dropped in the face of widespread opposition from pensioners living in the area and the television coverage that carried their message.

Other name proposals were to change the name of Coronation Street to Alf Roberts Street, but the Council secretly opined to Alf that such a name would be short-lived, as a road development was in the planning stage that sometime in the future would wipe out Coronation Street.

Another name proposed was Alf Roberts Wind (pronounced as in 'wind' the clock), but Audrey quashed that idea. 'Wind' could be crudely interpreted as 'wind', i.e. a bodily misdemeanour.

The most favoured tipple at the Rovers Return

Tastes have changed over the years. Once milk stout was consumed by the older denizens, though bitter is still popular with male drinkers. Females tend towards the 'new' drinks such as white wine and soda. Hilda Ogden had a penchant for

'Planter's Punch', a taste acquired from charring on a cruise ship. As a scene may require many takes, it would be unwise to serve the real stuff. The bitter is apparently a shandy and the lager is a shandy diluted with lemonade. Clear drinks are just plain water, and the darker drinks are a mixture of burnt sugar and water. Mike Baldwin's scotch is apple juice dispensed from a special optic, as Briggs does not like the burnt-sugar taste. Rarely the real thing is dispensed when the props room cannot concoct an imitation. As a rule the only real drinks would be mineral waters and fruit juices. Alf sticks with his pint of bitter, whilst his screen wife enjoys a gin and tonic.

Coronation Street Web pages

Granada TV's official *Coronation Street* Website:
  www.coronationstreet.co.uk/index.html
David A. Hannah's *Coronation Street* Home Page:
  http://home.echo-on.net/~buzzcorr/
Mike Plowman's *Coronation Street* Visual Updates Website:
  http://ds.dial.pipex.com/town/plaza/ec91
Graham Allsopp has a good *Street* site at
  http://www.shef.ac.uk/~gg1jga/street/
Bob's UK Unofficial *Coronation Street* Website:
  http//website.lineone./net~bob.r/

Film Web pages

Filmzone:
http://www.filmzone.com/february97/feb13.html
Entertainment on-line:
http://www.eonline.com/Facts/Movies/0,60,60045,00.html

The Granada Studios Tour

Granada Studios is a great place to visit, and even more so if you are a *Coronation Street* fan. You get to walk down the cobblestones of the Street itself, and to see some of the 'Reserve' sets that are occasionally used for filming when a storyline calls for heavy use of a particular set.

There are *Coronation Street* gift shops too, where you can buy everything from Newton and Ridley beer-mats to Bet Gilroy earrings! Included in the package price is a 'Backstage Tour', the Baker Street Set, UFO Zone, Motion Master, The Sooty Show, New York Street, The House of Commons Show, 3-D Shows, The Sound Effects Show, and The Horror-bly Squeamish Make-up Show!

There are lots of shops and places to eat and all of the usual facilities (toilets, baby-changing rooms and telephones) are available. It is wise to check the availablility of attractions (e.g. the *Street* set is not open every day), opening times and prices before you go. Telephone (0161) 832 9090 for more details. Postal address: Granada TV Studios, Quay Street, Manchester M60 9EA, United Kingdom.

In Canada, packages to England including a visit to Granada Tours can be arranged. Contact Katherine Semple at (416) 694 8234 or 1-800-743-3552.

The World of *Coronation Street*, Blackpool

If you are a fan of the *Street*, this is your dream come true. An unmissable opportunity to immerse yourself in the atmosphere and the history of the cobbled backstreet that has become a television legend.

You can explore a full-scale replica of the Street, walk through the famous sets and look behind the scenes of production control. At every turn, there are fascinating video presentations with the stars recalling treasured moments from the show. The whole experience is further enhanced by startling special effects and illusions.

Write to The World of *Coronation Street*, The Sandcastle, South Promenade, Blackpool, Lancashire, FY4 1BB. Tel: 01253 299555.

Magazine subscriptions

Subscriptions and back issues in Canada and the USA are
  available from: *Coronation Street*, PO Box 51545 RPO The
  Beaches, 2060 Queen Street East, Toronto, Ontario,
  Canada, M4E 3V7.
New Zealand and Australia: *Coronation Street Down Under*,
  Private Bag 92090, Auckland, New Zealand.
In the UK: *The Corner Shop*, The Official Magazine of
  Coronation Street, News-stand Publications, Office
  Block One, Southlink Business Park, Southlink, Oldham,
  OL4 1DE.

Coronation Street fan clubs

Canadian National Fan Club Director, c/o *Coronation Street*,
  PO Box 51545 RPO The Beaches, 2060 Queen Street
  East, Toronto, Ontario, Canada, M4E 3V7.
  Email: joanmctor.hookup.net
Information about The Official Magazine of *Coronation
  Street* which includes a free newsletter can be had by
  telephoning 416-694-8234 in the Toronto area or 1-800-

743-3552. John Briggs and Shirley Mansfield, 59-7501
Cumberland Street, Burnaby, V3N 4Y6, Canada. Email:
john_briggssfu.ca

Gail & Peter Drake, 2204 SE Lewellyn, Troutdale, OR USA
97060. Tel: (503) 666-8942. Fax: (503) 661-0429.

Rovers Hotpots, c/o Judith Tomlinson (Secretary), 10917-
85 Avenue Edmonton, AB, Canada, T6G 0W3.

Parksville-Qualicum Beach Club, Secretary: Betty Fraser, 999
Hollywood Road, Qualicum Beach, B.C., V9K 1N2.

Hamilton Club, President: Nancy Harris, 1003, 750 Mohawk
West Hamilton, ON L9C 5Z5.

Strathcona Streeties, President: (Bill Roberts), 649 Village
Drive, Sherwood Park, AB, T8A 4K7.

Coronation Street Friends, Eugenie Thoms, 105, 6880
Buswell Street, Richmond, B.C., V6Y 2Y7.

Vancouver Area Club, Dale Trigg, 1310 Tina Way, Port
Coquitlam, B.C., V3C 2V3. Email:
DALE_TRIGGbc.sympatico.ca

Streeters, Joan Byron, Apt. 116, 904 Clarke Road, Port
Moody, B.C., V3H 1L5.

Brantford Senior Streeters, Katherine Mary Gregory, 609,
640 West Street, Brantford, Ontario N3R 6M3.

South Surrey-White Rock Fan Club, Secretary: Joyce Wilks,
1664-157 Street, Surrey, B.C., V4A 4W3.

Calgary Streetalkers, President: Barbara Tiernay, 3611-1
Street N.W., Calgary, Alberta T2K 0W7.

Scarborough Ontario Fan Club, Jennifer Pickup (Secretary),
40 Mossbank Drive, Scarborough, Ontario, M1G 2C3.

Diabetes UK

Diabetes UK brings together in one place a wealth of information to assist people in the management and control of their diabetes. If your doctor recently diagnosed you with diabetes, you're not alone. There are nearly 1.5 million people in the United Kingdom with diabetes, with another estimated 1 million people who have not yet been diagnosed. That is, nearly one out of every 24 people have or could have diabetes. Visit the Website to find out what products and software are available to assist you.

Website: http://www.diabetic.org.uk

Email: diabetes-ukcableinet.co.uk

Marriage Encounter

Details of Marriage Encounter Weekends can be obtained by sending a stamped addressed envelope to: Peter and Irene Casey, Marriage Encounter, 4 Redclose Avenue, Morden, Surrey, SM4 5RD.

Christians In Entertainment

PO Box 17205, London SE26 4ZL.